Muammar Qaddafi

Other books in the People in the News series:

Muammar Qaddafi

By: Sheila Wyborny and Viqi Wagner

LUCENT BOOKS
A part of Gale, Cengage Learning

GALE
CENGAGE Learning·

Detroit • New York • San Francisco • New Haven, Conn • Waterville, Maine • London

GALE
CENGAGE Learning·

LIBRARY OF CONGRESS CATALOGING-IN-PUBLICATION DATA

Wyborny, Sheila, 1950-
  Muammar Qaddafi / by Sheila Wyborny and Viqi Wagner.
    p. cm. -- (People in the news)
  Includes bibliographical references and index.
    ISBN 978-1-4205-0759-1 (hardcover)
1. Qaddafi, Muammar--Juvenile literature. 2. Heads of state--Libya--Biography--Juvenile literature. 3. Soldiers--Libya--Biography--Juvenile literature. 4. Revolutionaries--Libya-Biography--Juvenile literature. 5. Libya--Politics and government--1969---Juvenile literature. I. Wagner, Viqi, 1953- II. Title.
    DT236.Q26W93 2013
    961.204'2092--dc23
    [B]
                                                                                      2012022864

Lucent Books
27500 Drake Rd
Farmington Hills MI 48331

ISBN-13: 978-1-4205-0759-1
ISBN-10: 1-4205-0759-1

Printed in the United States of America
1 2 3 4 5 6 7 16 15 14 13 12

Contents

Fame and celebrity are alluring. People are drawn to those who walk in fame's spotlight, whether they are known for great accomplishments or for notorious deeds. The lives of the famous pique public interest and attract attention, perhaps because their experiences seem in some ways so different from, yet in other ways so similar to, our own.

Newspapers, magazines, and television regularly capitalize on this fascination with celebrity by running profiles of famous people. For example, television programs such as *Entertainment Tonight* devote all their programming to stories about entertainment and entertainers. Magazines such as *People* fill their pages with stories of the private lives of famous people. Even newspapers, newsmagazines, and television news frequently delve into the lives of well-known personalities. Despite the number of articles and programs, few provide more than a superficial glimpse at their subjects.

Lucent's People in the News series offers young readers a deeper look into the lives of today's newsmakers, the influences that have shaped them, and the impact they have had in their fields of endeavor and on other people's lives. The subjects of the series hail from many disciplines and walks of life. They include authors, musicians, athletes, political leaders, entertainers, entrepreneurs, and others who have made a mark on modern life and who, in many cases, will continue to do so for years to come.

These biographies are more than factual chronicles. Each book emphasizes the contributions, accomplishments, or deeds that have brought fame or notoriety to the individual and shows how that person has influenced modern life. Authors portray their subjects in a realistic, unsentimental light. For example, Bill Gates—cofounder of the software giant Microsoft—has been instrumental in making personal computers the most vital tool of the modern age. Few dispute his business savvy, his perseverance, or his technical expertise, yet critics say he is ruthless in his dealings with competitors and driven more by his desire to maintain Microsoft's dominance in the computer industry than by an interest in furthering technology.

In these books, young readers will encounter inspiring stories about real people who achieved success despite enormous obstacles. Oprah Winfrey—one of the most powerful, most watched, and wealthiest women in television history—spent the first six years of her life in the care of her grandparents while her unwed mother sought work and a better life elsewhere. Her adolescence was colored by pregnancy at age fourteen, rape, and sexual abuse.

Each author documents and supports his or her work with an array of primary and secondary source quotations taken from diaries, letters, speeches, and interviews. All quotes are footnoted to show readers exactly how and where biographers derive their information and provide guidance for further research. The quotations enliven the text by giving readers eyewitness views of the life and accomplishments of each person covered in the People in the News series.

In addition, each book in the series includes photographs, annotated bibliographies, timelines, and comprehensive indexes. For both the casual reader and the student researcher, the People in the News series offers insight into the lives of today's newsmakers—people who shape the way we live, work, and play in the modern age.

Who Was the Real Qaddafi?

Muammar Qaddafi was dictator of Libya from 1969 to 2011. He was one of the most famous, and famously bizarre, political leaders of the modern age. His primary goal—power and influence in world politics and a place in history as a great man—was clear even before he seized control of the North African desert kingdom in 1969. But his story is confusing because he championed so many causes over so many years. As British expert in Libyan affairs Daniel Kawczynski writes, "Gaddafi was driven by such an enormous range of motives—exporting Libyan revolution, promoting Islam, working for Arab unity, restoring Palestinian territories [from Israel], opposing and undoing the deeds of Western colonialism—that his interventions had no meaningful pattern."[1]

The Many Personas of Qaddafi

Qaddafi pursued all these goals ruthlessly, with unwavering belief in his own abilities. In the process, he reinvented himself again and again.

First, he was a fanatical follower of Egyptian president Gamal Abdel Nasser, leader of the pan-Arab movement to create a single, united Arab state from the countries of North Africa and the Middle East. (Qaddafi envisioned himself at the head of this new state.) In this phase, Qaddafi told the Libyan people to forget about being Libyan and identify themselves

Muammar Qaddafi (left) with Egyptian President Gamal Abdel Nasser (center) in 1970. Qaddafi was a fanatical follower of Nasser.

as Arabs and Muslims with a common enemy—the European countries, the United States, and, most of all, the Jewish state of Israel.

At the same time, Qaddafi promoted himself as a Bedouin tribesman, son of a proud, nomadic ethnic group who was born in a desert tent. This persona of Qaddafi renounced wealth and worldly things and spent his time praying and thinking alone in the desert.

When the pan-Arab movement lost steam in the early 1970s, Qaddafi reinvented himself as a political philosopher and set out to transform Libya according to his own revolutionary theories. These theories, compiled in his famous three-volume Green Book, boiled down to *jamahiriyya,* a word Qaddafi invented that is usually translated as "statelessness." Qaddafi used it to mean a kind of pure democracy in which Libyans governed themselves with no political parties or elections, where profits and property belonged equally to everyone, and where no one was boss of anyone else. In practice, *jamahiriyya* gave Qaddafi unchallenged power to take what someone once owned—a business, a piece of land, a bank, a newspaper—and, in the name of the Libyan people and "equality," do whatever he wanted with it.

A Dictator Accountable to No One

The true source of Qaddafi's power was oil. Libya's vast oil reserves are the largest in Africa and the ninth largest in the world. Since its discovery in 1959, Libya's oil had been drilled and processed mostly by U.S. and British petroleum companies. Qaddafi nationalized the oil industry, then successfully reinvented himself as protector of an extremely profitable Libyan oil trade. He kept it running smoothly by allowing foreign companies to continue operations as long as they accepted all the risk and paid more for the oil.

With the Libyan treasury at his disposal, Qaddafi reinvented himself next as a supporter and sponsor of Libyan-style revolution elsewhere in the world. In this decades-long phase, he bankrolled so-called freedom fighters of all stripes. As defined by Qaddafi, freedom fighters ranged from terrorist groups such as the Irish Republican Army and the Fatah organization of Palestinian terrorist leader Abu Nidal to the African National Congress of Nelson Mandela, fighting the repressive, racist government of South Africa. Branded as a sponsor of international terrorism, Qaddafi became a political outcast in the West. The Libyan people suffered most during this phase, however; UN and U.S. trade bans crippled the Libyan economy, but Qaddafi continued to treat the treasury as his own personal bank.

In the mid-2000s, Qaddafi reinvented himself yet again; this time as a statesman and crisis-solver willing to cooperate with Europe and the United States. This political flexibility was a key factor in the dictator's ability to stay in power for so long. Accountable to no one and protected by a security network that turned Libya into a police state, he let others speculate about his true character while he did as he pleased.

Different Things to Different People

Supporters and underlings saw in Qaddafi a rational, shrewd politician, committed to his Green Book ideals. Revolutionaries around the world courted him and his deep pockets.

Political opponents cynically saw a cunning thug whose hodgepodge ideology was just a pretense to grab and hold power. In the Middle East and Africa, political leaders distrusted him as a loose cannon. They viewed him as a threat to their own power and stability. Western leaders such as U.S. president Ronald Reagan and British prime minister Margaret Thatcher made him out to be an evil genius—enemy number one—out to destroy their countries.

The international press, unable to make sense of his chaotic politics, oversimplified him as a madman and a buffoon. Most mass-distribution news stories focused on his idiotic eccentricities, his outlandish costumes and dyed hair, and his increasingly loose grasp of reality.

Indeed, the combination of his bullying outspokenness, petty vanity, and theatrics; his vast oil wealth; and his support of violent terrorist movements managed to give Libya a role on the

The international press often over-simplified Qaddafi by focusing on his eccentric clothing and behavior.

international stage far beyond that expected of an undeveloped country of 6 million people. Great ambition, however, did not lead to great achievements. "His pacts and unions crumbled, he often backed the loser, and he fell out badly with most of the states with which he dealt closely," noted Kawczynski in a 2011 biography of Qaddafi. "By the end of the 1980s, he had lost all credibility…. There was little respect for him left in the region, except, perhaps, for a grudging admiration for his willingness to speak bluntly."[2]

For Libyans, Qaddafi's emergence as a rehabilitated, enlightened leader in the late 2000s was too little, too late. In October 2011, Qaddafi fell as many dictators have fallen throughout history: by a humiliating and violent death at the hands of his own people. The man who wielded absolute power for more than forty years will be remembered for the ways he abused his power and for outrageous behavior that brought him the attention, but not the respect, he craved.

Chapter 1

A Child of Poverty in a Family of Wanderers

Muammar Qaddafi was born sometime between 1939 and 1942 in a desert region about twenty miles south of Sirte, a town by the Mediterranean Sea; however, the desert region of Qaddafi's birth is not the rolling dunes of golden sand portrayed in the silent-era films of Rudolph Valentino or the 1962 film epic *Lawrence of Arabia*. To the average eye, this desert is a forbidding, rocky, gray expanse of land with scrubby bushes. Understanding Qaddafi requires some knowledge of this region in which he was born. As Italian writer Mirella Bianco put it, "It is in the desert that one must seek the very essence of Gadafi nature, of the spirituality, of the mysticism which have greater weight than any of his aspirations, and which influence even his political action."[3]

Qaddafi's Berber Background

Summer in the desert is brutally hot and the winter is bitterly cold. Air conditioning to cool the intense summer heat is unheard of, nor do the people living in this region have central heating for the cold winters. In fact, most of the residents of the Libyan desert region have none of the modern conveniences of running water, electricity, or bathrooms with flushing toilets that most Westerners take for granted.

Muammar Qaddafi was born into a Berber tribe. The Berber people are desert dwellers, moving with their herds and living in goatskin tents.

To many people, this desert would appear an uninhabitable wasteland. In fact, most of Libya's population is concentrated in the towns and cities along the Mediterranean coastline. Small numbers of Libyans live in inland communities clustered around the oases. Not so for the Berber tribe into which Muammar Qaddafi was born. The Berber people are Bedouins; desert dwellers who are historically nomadic herders. Although today many Bedouin have settled in the cities, in Qaddafi's youth most Bedouin still moved with their herds from one grazing land to another, living in goatskin tents that they set up, took down, and transported with them. In kinship groups, they managed to survive under the most raw conditions and in the most desolate terrain in Libya's vast desert. Qaddafi once put the effect of desert dwelling on his life in the following way: "Bedouin society made me discover the natural laws, natural relationships, life in its true nature and what suffering was like before life knew oppression and exploitation."[4]

The Qaddafi family is a part of the Qaddafa tribe, a smaller kinship group within the Berber ethnic minority. According to Libyan politics scholar Geoff Simons, Qaddafa has an unsavory translation from Arabic: "those who spit out or vomit."[5] Like over

The Berber People

The history of Qaddafi's Berber people is rich and colorful. The Berbers have been a part of North Africa for thousands of years. Early Greeks, Romans, and Egyptians recorded their presence in the area as far back as 3,000 B.C. In fact, cave paintings in Libya dating back twelve thousand years have been attributed to early members of this group.

Prior to the eleventh century, much of northwestern Africa was populated by Berber-speaking Muslims. It was not until an invasion by an Egyptian tribe, the Banu Hilal, that the Berbers became Arabized in custom and language. It is interesting to note that Qaddafi, who is a Berber, sought an all-Arab state and for Libyans to identify themselves as Arabs. Historically, Berbers have resisted being grouped together with Arabs. They have rightly claimed that they occupied Libya long before their Arab conquerors came along. Yet, as an adult, Qaddafi expressed a hatred of Berbers, who were even persecuted under his regime.

Over time, the Berbers took on the traits, customs, and appearances of various invading groups. The physical appearances of the Berber people reflect this. For instance, skin tones can range from almost white to very dark brown, and their bodies are generally slender and slight.

Today, Berber people tend to live in rural areas and raise livestock, though some farm. Those Berbers who live in cities have stone homes, like city-dwellers of other groups. However, many who live in the smaller villages live in tents, just as their ancestors did.

95 percent of the Libyan people, the Qaddafi family is Muslim, members of the Islamic faith. Muslims follow the teachings of the Prophet Muhammad. As members of the Sunni sect, the largest in Islam, the Qaddafi family were among the most orthodox members of their faith. This means they followed the teachings of Muhammad to the letter, both in their religious observances and in all aspects of their daily lives.

"Nothing Between Us and the Sky"

Muammar Qaddafi's father was Mohammed Abdul Salam bin Hamed. He was also known by a much shorter name, Abu Meniar, translated as "father of the knife."[6] Like most of the men of his tribe, Abu Meniar was a goat and camel herder. He also worked at different times as a traveling merchant and a caretaker, whatever it took to support his family.

Qaddafi's mother was Aisha. According to some accounts, her family was originally Jewish but converted to Islam when Aisha was about nine years old. Like his father, Qaddafi's mother worked long, hard days to help her family survive the harsh living conditions of the desert. She also helped her husband pack their belongings and move when the herds had to be relocated from season-to-season.

Like many of the people of their tribe, neither Abu Meniar nor Aisha could read or write; however, this did not prevent

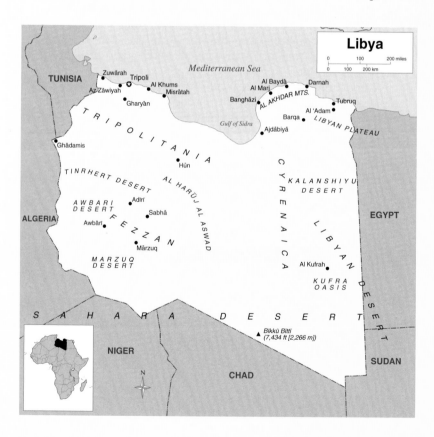

them from sharing the rich history and traditions of their people. They did this by telling their children the stories that were told to them by their own parents. By doing this, Qaddafi's parents helped keep the Berber traditions and history alive for another generation.

Qaddafi's mother died in 1978, when her son was in his late thirties. His father died seven years later, in 1985. Both had lived long enough to see their son become the absolute ruler of Libya and, for a variety of reasons, have his name known around the world.

The fact that Aisha and Abu Meniar's four children managed to survive infancy and childhood under the direst conditions is a success in its own right. Food was often scarce, and many children did not survive infancy. Qaddafi described the hardships and the advantages of his childhood in the following way:

> "It was difficult in terms of the circumstances and the environment under which I lived. Bedouin life is mobile; the strictness of upbringing therefore comes from the severity of these circumstances. But socially I was free. We were Bedouins enjoying full freedom and we lived amongst nature and everything was absolutely pure, in its true self, in front of us. We lived on the land and there was nothing between us and the sky."[7]

A Child of Troubled Times

Although Qaddafi's exact birth date is unknown, the most widely accepted year is 1942, and while he ruled Libya, official birthday celebrations took place on June 7.

His place of birth, however, has never been cause for dispute. He was born in the desert south of Sirte, a seaside town east of Tripoli. Occupied by Italy at that time, the Libyan coastline was sometimes referred to as Italy's "fourth coast."

Muammar was the youngest of four children and was the only son. One sister later died of cancer. Another sister married a man from Sirte, and the third married a man who became a local governor.

Benito Mussolini (standing) is shown touring Libya under Italian occupation in the 1934. A young Muammar Qaddafi grew up hearing stories about atrocities that were inflicted on the Libyan people during this time.

During his early childhood, Muammar learned the ways of his people, the Berber tribe, from his parents. His parents also provided some of his religious instruction, but much of what he learned about the Muslim faith came from local religious teachers. From his parents and his teachers he learned not only pride in his people and religion but also mistrust toward outsiders, particularly those who had invaded his country. He learned an Italian intruder murdered his grandfather in 1911 and that his own father and uncles had spent time in Italian jails.

According to reports, the Italian occupation was a time of much cruelty for Libyans. Civilian settlements were bombed, killing many children and old people. Women were raped and disemboweled. Men were forced onto airplanes, which were then flown to an altitude of over 1,300 feet (400m) over the desert. Once at that altitude, the men were pushed out of the planes, falling to their deaths, and the desert floor was littered with crumpled bodies. Berbers were starved to death in concentration camps. All in all, about twelve thousand Libyans were executed annually.

Qaddafi? Gadhafi? Kaddafi?

Throughout his decades in power, Libya's dictator's name appeared in print in a wide variety of English spellings: *Gadaffi, Gathafi, Gaddafi, Kaddafi, Qaddafi, Qadhafi, and Khadafy*, just to name a few. In fact, in 2009, ABC News researcher Sadie Bass was able to come up with 112 spellings of the Libyan ruler's name. There are also some variations in the spelling of his first name: Muammar and Moammar, for example. Qaddafi's family name is also sometimes prefaced with the article "el" or "al." In the mid-1980s, either Qaddafi or some of his staff used "Moammar el-Gadhafi" as his official signature. The addition of "el" to his surname was said to come across as more important, more official.

One reason for the multiple spellings has to do with the way Arabic is translated into English. There is no universally recognized method, so variation is common. Additionally, the dictator himself, for whatever reason, provided no "official" pronunciation of his name and seemed to add to the translation confusion: His own official website referred to him by at least four different spellings. Following the style adopted by major newspapers such as the *New York Times*, this book goes with Muammar Qaddafi, a spelling no more nor less authoritative than any other.

Young Muammar grew up hearing stories of such atrocities, which only intensified his hatred toward outsiders. Finally, though, the Italians as well as the other Axis powers were defeated in World War II, and the Italian invaders were forced out. Libya became to some extent an independent country.

First School Days

About the time Libya was achieving its independence from outside rule and establishing its own monarchy, Muammar began his formal education at a primary school in Sirte. He became the first member of his family to go to school and learn to read and write. He was a little older than the other boys in his classes, and his family sacrificed from their meager income in order to send him to school. During the week, he slept on the floor of a local mosque. On Thursdays, the beginning of the Muslim weekend, he walked through the desert to be with his family and once again sleep in the tent that was the family home. Then, on Friday evening, Muammar returned to the city to resume his studies.

Muammar's parents and teachers knew he was a very intelligent child. From the beginning of his education, he was a hard-working, serious student; however, being a good student did not make his life easy. During his earlier school days, some of his classmates looked down on him. They made fun of him because his family was poor and lived in the desert. Muammar did not allow their rude treatment to bring him down. Instead, this young child, not yet in his teens, won over his classmates with his wit and charm. Before long, he was one of the top students both academically and socially. Muammar was between eight and ten when he began primary school and about fourteen when he finished.

The Revolutionary Seed Is Planted

When Muammar finished primary school in Sirte, his family moved to the town of Sebha, in the Fezzan region, so he could continue his education. His secondary school years were not easy ones, either. To be near his son, Muammar's father temporarily gave up being a herder and worked as a caretaker on the property of a local tribal leader, two miles from town. During this time, the family lived in a shack, rather than a tent. As he did in primary school, every Thursday evening Muammar made a long walk to be with his family.

At secondary school, Muammar quickly impressed his teachers with his intelligence and diligence toward his studies. One teacher took note of the boy and his studious habits, saying that Muammar was "gifted, conscientious and solitary, with a sobriety bordering on asceticism."[8]

Another teacher recalled a note Muammar once gave him. In the note were questions about revolutions and how to organize a government; complicated ideas for one so young, and quite

When Muammar Qaddafi finished primary school, his family moved to the town of Sebha so he could continue his education.

foretelling: "What is a pyramid organization and which is the best manner to organize such a structure?" he wrote. "Does the possibility of organizing a revolution in Libya exist? If a revolution were to be carried out in Libya, would Egypt come to the assistance of the Libyan people?"[9]

The teacher, Mohamoud Efay, an Egyptian, was as thoughtful with his answers as his young student was with his questions. He told the boy that any revolution would have to be carefully thought out with regard to organizing the various departments of a new government. He also said it would not be possible without the support of an army.

Qaddafi Is Expelled

Nonetheless Muammar's thoughts of revolution continued. While he remained serious about his studies, over time he became more outspoken. He was older than many of his classmates, and they respected him. In fact, some of his friends from his secondary school days remained close to him until the end of his life. Many of his boyhood friends remember him as a student revolutionary. He would stand on a stool or a wall in the school's garden and make speeches about the government and what needed to be done to make Libya a better country for its people. He was a convincing speaker and swayed many students to his point of view.

After a time, Muammar went from speech making to planning and carrying out demonstrations. He led his fellow students in political marches. This brought him to the attention of local law enforcement. In 1961, after several protests, some of which resulted in property damage, such as broken windows, the police finally went to the school administrators and informed them of Muammar's activities.

A document signed by the minister of education and sent to the school's headmaster clearly spelled out the consequences of Muammar's actions: "With reference to the report submitted by you the deputy principal of Sebha central school and the controller of the boarding section concerning the students who led the 5 October 1961 demonstration I convey to you the penalties which we deemed necessary to be applied against the following students:

1) Muammar Abu Meniar al Qaddafi discharged from the school and prevented from studying at the schools of the state."[10] Muammar may have believed his behavior was political activism, but it was considered treasonable behavior by the authorities.

The Actions of a Desperate Father

Muammar's father, Abu Meniar, was very upset by this turn of events. He wanted his son to finish secondary school, but being expelled from the Sebha school was only one of the problems. The other was Muammar's age. Since he was older when he began school, he was already around nineteen at the time of his expulsion. Most young men of his age were already working or at university. Additionally, secondary schools were not compelled to enroll a student that old.

His father enlisted the help of his employer in finding a secondary school that would accept Muammar. Then, since his son was too old to enroll in secondary school with his legal birth certificate, Abu Meniar took the actions of a desperate father. He talked a local official into providing Muammar with falsified birth records, which declared him a couple of years younger than he actually was. This is one of the issues that lead to confusion over his birth date. With his falsified birth certificate, the young revolutionary enrolled in a secondary school in the town of Misrata.

Early Influences

Muammar did not develop his revolutionary ideas on his own. He was influenced by revolutionaries who had gone before him. Egyptian leader Gamal Abdel Nasser was perhaps his greatest hero. Muammar was especially impressed by Nasser because he had formed a group called the Free Unionist Officers Movement, and had removed the Egyptian king, Farouk, in 1952.

When he had gone off to school, Muammar's tribe had given him a small transistor radio. He did not use his radio for entertainment, though. He listened to learn. He was especially impressed by Radio Cairo and the program *Voice of the Arabs*. This is where he first heard Nasser speak. He became so obsessed with Nasser's speeches that he would sometimes go without food in order to use the little money he had to buy batteries for his radio. He did not want to miss even one of Nasser's speeches. He even went so far as to memorize them word-for-word.

Muammar also read Nasser's only book, *Philosophy of the Revolution*, first published in 1955, which was like a guidebook for how to organize a revolution. To young Muammar, Nasser's book was second only to the Koran (the Islamic holy book) in importance. The prose was dramatic and enticing for a teenager. In his book, Nasser described in simple and compelling terms the life of a revolutionary: "Our life during that period [as they plotted the revolution] was like a thrilling detective story. We had dark secrets and passwords. We lurked in the shadows, we had caches of pistols and hand-grenades, and firing bullets was our cherished hope. We made many attempts in this direction and I can still remember our emotions and feelings as we dashed along that melodramatic path."[11]

Nasser's words also fueled Muammar's pride in being an Arab. "When I try to analyse the elements of our strength there are three main sources: the first is that we are a community of neighboring

Gamal Abdel Nasser was Muammar Qaddafi's greatest role model. He read Nasser's book and listened faithfully to his speeches, even going as far as memorizing them word for word.

peoples linked by all the material and moral ties possible," wrote Nasser. "The second is our land itself and its position on the map. The third is oil, a sinew of material civilization without which all its machines would cease to function."[12] Young Muammar absorbed Nasser's words and all their meaning.

Hating King Idris

Muammar was also influenced—though in a negative way—by King Idris I, Libya's leader. Idris I was the direct opposite of Nasser. He tried to walk a narrow line between the Muslim/Arab world and the West—not too successfully, according to those who idolized Nasser.

Muammar was taught from early childhood that faithful Muslims do not drink, dance, smoke, gamble, or have sex before marriage. Although Idris was from a respected Muslim family, some said he did not follow the faith's strict rules of behavior. Whether the king participated in these activities or not, he allowed drinking and gambling in the country. Muammar believed that by allowing these behaviors, the king was damaging the country and contaminating its culture.

Additionally, under King Idris, Libya was heavily dependent on Western countries, particularly the United States and Great Britain. In fact, it was Great Britain that had helped him become the king of Libya. Idris I allowed both the United States and Great Britain to have military bases on Libyan land. He also allowed their airplanes to practice bombing runs in the Libyan desert. The money both countries paid Libya to host their military bases was a major source of income for Libya at that time.

Despite the fact that Libya prospered under Idris, Muammar, because of his lifelong hatred and distrust of outsiders, did not believe that the United States or Great Britain should have access to any Libyan land. This, too, caused the young student to distrust his country's leader. Because of the king's ties to the West, Muammar felt Idris was little more than a puppet in the hands of Western leaders, whom he despised.

Muammar graduated from secondary school sometime between 1961 and 1963 (sources, including Qaddafi himself, report varying dates for many of the events of his youth). In only about six years, he would lead a coup that would make him the leader of Libya—however, he had a few more years of education as well as military training ahead of him before he could achieve his goal.

Chapter 2

The Making of a Revolutionary

When Qaddafi started primary school, Libya was a very poor country, supported in part by money from the United States and Great Britain for their military bases. By the time he started university, though, Libya's economy had changed dramatically. In the mid-1950s, oil was discovered in the Algerian portion of the Sahara Desert, prompting oil companies to begin prospecting in the Libyan Desert. The first oil strike in Libya was near Bir Zelten in April 1959, and many others followed. In a few short years, Libya had morphed from a poverty-stricken nation into an oil-rich one. The young Qaddafi, however, saw little of that wealth trickle down to the very poor of his country. Instead, it remained in the hands of King Idris I and his already wealthy supporters. The injustice of this situation frustrated Qaddafi as he moved from high school to university.

University and Cadet Days

After high school graduation, Qaddafi enrolled in the University of Libya in Tripoli. Established in 1955, the university had a connection to Qaddafi's hero, Gamal Abdel Nasser, Egypt's prime minister at the time the university was founded. At the request of the Libyan government, Nasser sent four lecturers to the new university and even funded their salaries for several years.

Muammar Qaddafi (right) is shown praying in the desert. As a student enrolled in the University of Libya, Qaddafi followed strict Muslim habits, like observing prayer times, and inspired his student followers to do the same.

While at the university, Qaddafi studied political science and history as well as the ideologies of Marxism and communism. At first he majored in law but chose to take advantage of the military training offered at the university. As a student leader, he continued his speech making and protesting, and he encouraged other students to join him in protesting what he saw as the failings of the government. He also inspired his followers to follow strict Muslim habits, such as observing prayer times, avoiding alcohol and gambling, and abstaining from sex until marriage.

Qaddafi chose not to complete his law studies. Instead, he applied to the Benghazi Military Academy. Although his protest activities could have caused his application to be rejected, it has been said that his excellent grades at the university assured him of admission. According to some stories, Qaddafi and some of his most trusted friends enrolled in the academy not to learn how to serve and protect the current government, but rather to recruit others to join them in putting together a plan to overthrow the regime of Idris I.

King Idris I

Throughout his high school, university, and cadet days, Qaddafi had one goal: removing Idris I from power. The man targeted for so long by Qaddafi was named Sidi Muhammad Idris al-Mahdi as-Sanusi. He ruled Libya from 1951 until Qaddafi's coup in 1969.

As a young man, Idris headed an Islamic mystic sect, the Sanusiyah, and rose to become emir (a Muslim leader, or sheikh) of Cyrenaica, the vast province that makes up the eastern half of modern-day Libya. Cyrenaica sided with the British and American Allies against Italy and Germany, the Axis powers, in World War II. After the war, with British and United Nations backing, Cyrenaica and the western provinces of Tripolitania and Fezzan that had made up an Italian colony were united as one independent nation—the United Kingdom of Libya. Idris became Libya's first (and only) king. He had absolute control of its military and a great deal of control over its parliament.

Idris I believed his poor country would not be able to survive without help from the West, so he pursued agreements and ventures with Great Britain and the United States. Over time, oil revenues began to enrich Libya's treasury.

Between Idris I's association with the West and what many saw as his keeping oil wealth in the hands of the already wealthy, many younger Libyans, including Muammar Qaddafi, began seeking ways to remove him from power. After the 1969 coup that brought Qaddafi to power, Idris went into exile in Egypt. Sentenced to death in absentia by Qaddafi's Libyan People's Court in 1971, Idris never returned to Libya. He died peacefully in Cairo in 1983, at the age of ninety-four.

"Our Most Backward Cadet"

From the outset, Qaddafi was not impressed by some of his fellow cadets. Many of them came from wealthy families and seemed spoiled. Rather than behave as serious cadets and good Muslims, many of them gambled, drank, and chased women—all activities strictly forbidden by Islamic law. Because of their behavior, Qaddafi avoided these cadets. Instead, he associated with cadets who, like himself, were devout Muslims. They came from poor families, as he did, maintained strong family ties, and above all avoided what he referred to as godless, decadent behavior.

Qaddafi's attitude did not go unnoticed, and it affected his success while at the academy. British officer Colonel Ted Lough remembered Qaddafi as a student. "He was our most backward cadet," noted Lough; "98 percent of the cadets passed their exams, 2 percent failed, and he was one of them. He was probably not as stupid as I thought at the time. Part of his problem was that he wouldn't learn English. I didn't like him and he made life difficult for my officers and men because he went out of his way to be rude to them."[13]

Rudeness and the refusal to learn English were not the only issues Qaddafi had. Qaddafi biographers David Blundy and Andrew Lycett interviewed an academy officer (who refused to be identified to avoid reprisals) who told them of an incident involving a cadet who may have been accused of a sexual offense, possibly homosexuality: "Qaddafi and a couple of the others started firing at him, or playing with him, really. They fired to the right, then to the left. The bloke [guy] was running this way and that. Then they shot him. The officer went over, took out his revolver, and gave him the *coup de grâce* [a finishing shot to end the victim's suffering].... They left the body lying there and then they kind of celebrated. They were all laughing."[14]

A Growing Opposition to the King

During the time Qaddafi was in school and at the military academy, political tensions ran high throughout Libya. Qaddafi was not the only one unhappy with the current regime. One government

King Idris (pictured) made several highly unpopular decisions, causing opposition towards him to grow over the years. Qaddafi numbered among the many Libyan citizens who were unhappy with the King Idris regime.

decision, made in 1953, was particularly unpopular. Idris had agreed to a twenty-year treaty with Great Britain, which allowed the extensive use of Libyan land in return for financial assistance.

He signed a similar agreement with the United States, in 1954, for the use of Wheelus Air Base (now Mitiga International Airport) just outside of Tripoli. In return, the United States agreed to provide technical, financial, and military assistance.

Also unpopular was the presence of outside oil companies on Libyan soil. Many of the Westerners who worked for these companies participated in un-Islamic activities, such as drinking and gambling; however, in order to keep the Western workers happy—and willing to work in Libya—Idris looked the other way and tolerated behavior that Muslim law forbade. Religious Libyans resented him for this and also for the way he used the money that poured in from the oil industry. He spent these funds on himself, his family, and friends; none of it went to average or poor Libyans. The combination of these issues led to considerable unrest that continued to grow over the years that Idris was in power.

Another of the king's earlier moves was to ban all political opposition. Antigovernment Libyans, therefore, had to operate undercover, below the government's radar. To show open involvement in opposition groups could have dire consequences. The most active of these underground groups were the Muslim Brothers, the Baathists, and the Nasserites, which was the most popular group.

Demonstrations

By January 1964, while Qaddafi was still a cadet, tensions led to the outburst of student demonstrations in the cities of Tripoli and Benghazi. Qaddafi participated in some of these protests and honed his personality traits that inspired leadership. He was extremely charismatic, which enabled him to persuade many fellow cadets to follow his lead. They did as he asked with absolute trust and loyalty. In fact, the protest group he led during those days was so successful that, although as individuals they were simply considered random troublemakers, they were never detected as a group by the police.

Though some of his personality traits attracted his fellow students and cadets, others did not. He was charming and encouraging—as long as others did his bidding. If anyone crossed him, disagreed with him, or behaved in ways he thought inappropriate or un-Islamic, his behavior was quite different. He was rude and arrogant toward his instructors when he disagreed with their lectures. When it came to some of his peers, he was downright cruel and sometimes even sadistic, as evidenced by his part in the shooting of one of his fellow cadets.

Qaddafi's personality was complex indeed. As author Lillian Craig Harris puts it, "The psychological complexity of Qadhafi's character appears to indicate that his need for acceptance … arises not from feelings of inferiority but from a belief in his own superiority and his anger at the failure of others to recognize it."[15] Harris's observations describe a person determined to be in charge at all costs. His actions as a student, a cadet, and later as an army officer lend credibility to this description.

Early Military Career

After two years at the academy, Qaddafi finished his training in about 1965 and was commissioned as a lieutenant in the Libyan Army upon graduation. He first applied for a four-month training program in the United States, but his government denied him permission to go. Next, he applied for a six-month training program in England. This was for training for the special Signal Corps, the units responsible for military communications using radio, radar, and satellite signals.

Qaddafi did not apply for these programs because he wanted to experience life outside of Libya; in fact, he hated all Western influence. Rather, he wanted to study abroad to learn the latest and most sophisticated military techniques. The only place to get this training was in a Western country. He was granted permission to go to England and was accepted for that training program, which surprised Col. Ted Lough, who did not trust Qaddafi's motives. "I can't understand it. He must have slipped through the net,"[16] Lough said at the time.

In England, Qaddafi was sent to Beaconsfield for his Signal Corps training. While there, he also learned English, a language he had for years refused to learn because of his contempt for Western ways. Despite this, he built a rapport with his English teacher and later even sent him a Christmas card. After his time in Beaconsfield,

Qaddafi completed his military training in England in 1966 and then returned to Libya where he was commissioned in the Libyan Army Signal Corps.

Qaddafi moved to Dorset where he studied communications and learned how to fire tank guns. According to people acquainted with him at that time, he did not seem to enjoy his training period in England but rather treated it as something he had to do, a step in the process, in order to accomplish his goals.

Upon completing his training in England in 1966, Qaddafi returned to Libya where he was commissioned in the Libyan Army Signal Corps. He was posted to a base near Benghazi, Libya's second-largest city and a major seaport on the Gulf of Sidra. His agenda had nothing to do with serving and protecting the existing government, though. He sought to overthrow the government of Idris I. He held secret meetings and recruited supporters to his cause; at one point, his "secret" personal army numbered more than seven thousand members. The group was never identified by the king's secret police; Qaddafi's Western training helped assure that rebel communications were not intercepted.

The core group of Qaddafi's coconspirators, mostly former schoolmates, was a band of about a hundred junior army officers known as the Free Officers' Movement. They, like Qaddafi, dreamed of overthrowing Idris I and creating a pan-Arab (all-Arab) state—the unification of the Arabic-speaking countries of North Africa and the Middle East— governed from Libya by Libyans. While they plotted their revolution, something happened in 1967 that, at least for a time, seriously dampened the morale of Qaddafi and his followers.

A Pivotal Summer

Since the creation of the State of Israel in 1948, hostilities had intensified between the new Jewish state and its predominantly Muslim Arab neighbors, Egypt, Jordan, and Syria. Border skirmishes between Israel and neighboring Arab countries, which were fundamentally opposed to Israel's existence, increased in the mid-1960s.

In May 1967, Nasser received reports from the Soviet Union that Israel was staging a troop concentration on Syria's border. Although the reports later turned out to be untrue, Nasser began a troop buildup on the Sinai Peninsula, which borders Israel, and took up an advantageous position overlooking the Straits of Tiran. He also closed the straits to Israeli ships, which, according to a 1957 declaration, could constitute an act of war. Jordan, Iraq, and Syria also made troop movements and defense agreements that indicated a confrontation was brewing.

Finally, after much military jockeying and posturing, on June 5, 1967, Israel launched a series of surprise air strikes against the Arab military forces poised at its borders. This event came to be known as the Arab-Israeli War, or the Six-Day War. Even though Arab forces greatly outnumbered the Israelis, Israel swiftly captured the Gaza Strip and the Sinai Peninsula from Egypt, as well as territories from Jordan and Syria. By June 11, a cease-fire was signed and the war was over: Israel emerged militarily and politically victorious, while Nasser and the other Arab forces had suffered a humiliating defeat.

Whether Israel acted too aggressively, or whether it was justly defending itself, is a matter of heated debate. In Qaddafi's opinion, it was an act of aggression. The Arab defeat—as well as the defeat of his boyhood hero, Nasser—shocked Qaddafi. It was a depressing time for him and his followers, who viewed Nasser as the ultimate Arab leader and essentially undefeatable. Qaddafi did not waste

The New Leader Gets Lost

Although the coup that left Qaddafi leader of Libya was a very serious event, it was marked by a number of almost comical moments. For example, the officer Qaddafi put in charge of taking over the radio station got lost en route, unable to find the facility. He made his way back to the barracks in a panic. Another officer who knew the route finally drove him to the radio station.

Qaddafi himself got turned around in the chaos. In a rare show of self-deprecation, he described how he suddenly found himself alone, without his supporters, right in the middle of the coup: "I jumped into my jeep and drove to the head of my column. I took the Jilyana road as planned and then took a left fork. The vehicles following me, which were supposed to come with me to occupy the radio station [in Benghazi], well, they went straight on at full speed heading for Berka. I found myself alone in my jeep, bowling along the road to Benghazi, no lights, nothing."

Quoted in David Blundy and Andrew Lycett. *Qaddafi and the Libyan Revolution.* London: Weidenfeld and Nicolson, 1987, p. 58.

much time licking his wounds, however. Instead, he focused his attention on covertly preparing for his own military action.

Qaddafi Makes His Move

By 1969, Idris I was in failing health. The king delegated more and more official duties to his nephew and designated heir, Crown Prince Hasan as-Sanusi. In August, Idris announced his abdication: he would step down on September 2, and Hasan would take the throne as king of Libya. Then Idris and his wife left Libya for medical treatment in Turkey.

Qaddafi and his coconspirators decided to make their move. On September 1, 1969, under the guise of a training exercise, Qaddafi's followers raided the royal palace. Scattered groups of

On September 1, 1969, Qaddafi led a successful, bloodless coup that overthrew the Idris regime. The young, confidant, but still unknown Muammar Qaddafi was suddenly in charge.

supporters moved to positions elsewhere in Tripoli, Benghazi, and smaller towns throughout Libya. They took over the Benghazi radio station, the only mass communications facility for most of Libya. There, they broadcast condemnation of the king and also called for Arab unity, especially against what they referred to as the enemy of Islam, their term for Israel.

At five o'clock that morning, Peter Wakefield, the consul-general for the British embassy in Benghazi, was walking the deserted streets toward home, having spent the night sending coded messages to London about disturbances in Libya that indicated a coup d'etat (a sudden overthrow of the government) might be imminent. He encountered a group of armed young men, carrying weapons. They politely asked him to accompany them to the local radio station. There, they introduced him to another young man, very neatly turned out in a freshly pressed army uniform. The dapper young man was Muammar Qaddafi,

An American Child's Memory of Qaddafi's Coup

Some Western families were living in Libya at the time of the 1969 coup. Many of them were involved in the oil industry. American Ron McWhorter, a child at the time, related his impressions of life in Libya at the time of the relatively quiet coup:

> On September 1, it was the first day of school for all of us who attended the Oil Company School (OCS). Thousands of students and mostly American teachers were brought over by the oil companies. My mom was so glad to get rid of me and my sisters, since we fought all summer. My dad decided to drive us to school that day, just a few blocks away. Normally, we'd walk. Well, several people came out of their houses to stop us, reporting there was trouble downtown. We turned around and my mom said, "What the heck are you doing back?" We were under strict curfew for about six weeks.

Ron McWhorter. E-mail interview with Sheila Wyborny, July 12, 2011.

who had come to the radio station to inform the country that he and his followers had overthrown the Idris regime. Wakefield was the first foreign official to meet the new leader.

Instead of going home, Wakefield returned to his office and dashed off a telegram to London, simply stating that this unknown young man, Qaddafi, had taken control of the country. At that point, no one knew enough about Qaddafi to have any idea of how he intended to conduct himself as leader.

The bloodless coup, the event that would chart the course for Libya for over four decades, was over within a few short hours. Libya had a new man in charge, and people within the country were understandably fearful. He was virtually unknown, so no one knew what to expect from him.

Chapter 3

Building a Dictatorship

Suddenly in charge of a nation, Qaddafi wasted no time enacting his revolutionary reforms. In one sense he was remarkably successful. He did what he set out to do: transform the Libyan economy and government, Libyans' way of life, and Libya's relations with other countries. But as Qaddafi's chaotic social and political experiments stripped Libyans of one freedom after another, it became clear that the one who benefited most was Qaddafi himself.

An Astonishingly Easy Coup

On the day of the coup, the twenty-seven-year-old Qaddafi announced Libya's regime change in a radio broadcast to the nation. The ranting style he would soon be famous for was already apparent: "People of Libya. In response to your own will, fulfilling your most heartfelt wishes … your armed forces have undertaken the overthrow of the reactionary and corrupt regime, the stench of which has sickened and horrified us all, [and] which was no more than a hotbed of extortion, faction, treachery, and treason."[17]

Qaddafi shrewdly realized that the legitimacy of the new regime depended on quick recognition by the king's foreign allies. He therefore made sure his first speech included reassuring words for U.S. and British military and oil company personnel in Libya: "I have pleasure in assuring all our foreign friends that they need

Muammar Qaddafi addressing the Libyan people through a radio broadcast on the day of the coup in 1969.

have no fears either for their property or for their safety. They are under the protection of our armed forces.... Our enterprise is in no sense directed against any state whatever, nor against international agreements."[18]

Finally, Qaddafi announced the country's new name—the Libyan Arab Republic—and promised the Libyan people a golden age: "[Libya] will advance on the road to freedom, the path of unity and social justice, guaranteeing equality to all her citizens and throwing wide in front of them the gate of honest employment, where injustice and exploitation are banished, where no one will count himself master and servant, and where all will be free."[19]

That same day, Crown Prince Hasan broadcast his own message, giving up all claims to the throne and pledging to support the new government. Four days later, Idris I issued a statement from Turkey that he had not much enjoyed being king anyway and, in any case, had already abdicated the throne. Within three days of the coup, local police forces and a few army units loyal to the king had surrendered. Egypt, Iraq, Syria, and Sudan recognized the new government immediately. Britain and the United States, eager to protect their oil drilling operations, decided to cooperate with the new regime. Western and Middle Eastern governments, assuming a few senior military leaders had taken over, waited for the next official announcements.

Qaddafi: First Among Equals

Foreign countries were surprised to learn that the coup leaders were young officers from Libya's lower class, with no ties to the king or his army's top brass. They should not have been so surprised. Decades of brutal occupation by Italy had made Libyans second-class citizens in their own country. Many were illiterate and poor. There were not many educated, qualified people in the king's government; the ambitious young men of the Free Officers' Movement simply moved in to fill the vacuum. The real leader of the coup, however, was Qaddafi. On September 8, Qaddafi was promoted to colonel, the highest rank in the Libyan army, and named commander in chief of the armed forces.

Adopting the motto Freedom, Socialism, and Unity, Qaddafi announced the creation of a twelve-member governing body, the Revolutionary Command Council (RCC), which he declared would share decision making. Then he named himself chairman of the RCC and delayed naming its other members for four months. In short order, Qaddafi arrested the council's minister of defense and minister of the interior, charged them with plotting against him, and assumed their titles. Over the next decade he gave himself a number of additional titles, including Secretary-General of the General People's Congress of Libya, Prime Minister of Libya, and Brotherly Leader and Guide of the Revolution of Libya.

The Qaddafi Family

Qaddafi's personal life was not widely publicized. He preferred to promote a public image of a solitary thinker praying in the desert. In fact, he married twice and had ten children, some of whom became nearly as notorious as himself.

Qaddafi's first wife was a schoolteacher named Fatiha, whom he reportedly married in the late 1960s without first meeting her. Their son, Muhammad, was born in 1970.

Soon after that, Qaddafi divorced Fatiha and married Safia Farkash, who was already pregnant with their first child, son Saif al-Islam. Safia bore five more sons—Saadi, Mutassim, Hannibal, Saif al-Arab, and Khamis—and one daughter, Aisha. The couple later adopted a nephew, Milad, as their son, and a daughter, Hana.

Qaddafi appointed several of his adult children to vaguely defined but very lucrative positions in charge of Libyan telecommunications, real estate, arms deals, construction, and foreign investments. Eldest son Muhammad, for example, controlled Libya's cell phone and satellite networks (and was head of Libya's Olympic Committee). Saif al-Islam was his father's chosen successor; educated at the London School of Economics, he spoke English fluently. Daughter Aisha, a lawyer, was a very vocal supporter of her father and his sponsorship of international terrorists/revolutionaries and a member of the legal defense team of Iraqi dictator Saddam Hussein after the latter was captured by U.S.-led forces in the Iraq War. Mutassim was Qaddafi's national security adviser, and Khamis commanded a special forces brigade, known as the Khamis Brigade, that was blamed for some of the most brutal crackdowns on Libyan civilians during the 2011 uprising.

The RCC, with Qaddafi at its head, took control of nearly all government ministries. Any government officials or Libyan diplomats with links to the king were fired or arrested; Hasan was imprisoned for three years, then forced to live with his family in cabins on a public beach.

Ousting the Westerners

For the first four to five years after the coup, Qaddafi zealously preached pan-Arabism, the philosophy of his idol, Nasser of Egypt. Its basic principles were Libyans' kinship and alliance with North African and Middle Eastern countries, hatred of Israel

Muammar Qaddafi (left) shaking hands with Egypt's Prime Minister, Gamal Abdel Nasser, in 1969. For the first few years after the coup Qaddafi preached pan-Arabism, the philosophy of his idol Nasser.

and Western influence, and the restoration of the Arab world to its historical greatness.

Despite his early assurances, Qaddafi took immediate action against Westerners in Libya. Within a year, he had ousted British and U.S. military troops and closed their bases. Then, in 1970, he partly nationalized, or put under state control, the oil industry, which he named the National Oil Corporation. Qaddafi needed foreign technical expertise to run the oil operations, however, so he allowed foreign companies such as Shell and British Petroleum to continue working after renegotiating contracts that quadrupled Libya's oil income.

Ron McWhorter, whose father was working in Libya during the coup, remembers how relations between Libyans and Westerners changed: "After the revolution, there was a noticeable chill between the Americans and Libyans. Not as much contact, for sure…. The ban on alcohol by Qaddafi was quite a problem and, of course, the ex-pats [Libyans living abroad] and Italians weren't happy. The only exemption I know was for all the Americans, Brits, and Canadians working on drilling and seismic crews in the desert. They all threatened to quit if they couldn't have alcohol!"[20]

The Arab Socialist Union

Qaddafi also moved quickly to create a partial pan-Arab union among Libya, Egypt, and Sudan called the Federation of Arab Republics. That short-lived experiment failed for several reasons. First, Nasser died in late 1970, and his successor, Anwar Sadat, did not like or trust Qaddafi. The Syrian president likewise resisted the idea of giving up his own power to anyone, let alone Qaddafi. Then the Arab world in general was humiliated in 1973 when Israel defeated a surprise Arab military attack. In the aftermath, the pan-Arab movement fizzled, and Qaddafi was brushed aside.

According to Libyan affairs expert Dirk Vandewalle, "Within … the Arab world at large, Gadhafi didn't really have the kind of stature he thought he had…. He started to abandon Arab nationalism. He lashed out against Arab leaders, in part because ... they were snickering behind his back. He was considered, in a sense, a country bumpkin by many of the Arab leaders. And at that point, the [Libyan] revolution really kind of turn[ed] internal."[21]

Dismantling the Government

His pan-Arab ambitions thwarted, Qaddafi set out to put his radical ideas in action inside Libya. On April 15, 1973, he delivered a shocking five-point address in Zuwarah, suspending all laws, announcing a purge of the "politically sick"[22] (meaning critics of his regime), creating a people's militia, and declaring both administrative and cultural revolution. With this address, Qaddafi assumed absolute power.

In 1973, Qaddafi announced some radical new changes coming to Libya. He created a people's militia, changed government policies, greatly increased surveillance on the Libyan people, all to ensure he would assume and hold absolute power over his country.

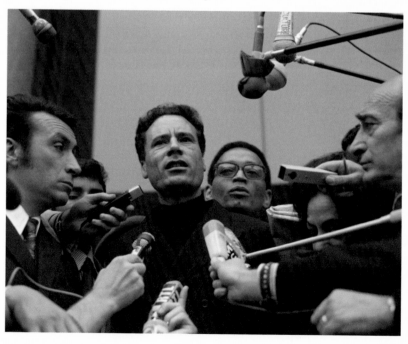

Political parties, elections, and trade unions were banned, replaced by some twenty-six hundred local Revolutionary Committees, which, Qaddafi argued, would allow Libyans to rule themselves and solve their own disagreements. In truth, this political participation was just for show. It served three purposes. First, Qaddafi could point to local committees as pure democracy, proof that Libyans managed their own affairs and that he encouraged his people to voice their opinions. But local committees had no real say in central decision making, which rested in Qaddafi and a small group of trusted advisers. Second, splitting local government into small, fragmented groups was an effective divide-and-conquer tactic. Set against one another, the local groups fell to petty squabbling that undermined organized opposition. Third, the Revolutionary Committees were ideal surveillance tools. Staffed with police agents and Qaddafi informants—up to 20 percent of Libyans worked in surveillance—they rigidly enforced Qaddafi's policies and spied on potential dissenters at long, tedious meetings citizens were forced to attend.

With no elected national officials or courts, there was no system of checks and balances on Qaddafi's power and no way to remove him from power. What he called pure democracy was the beginning of autocracy.

Dismantling Civil Society

With absolute control of government, Qaddafi set out to revolutionize (that is, dismantle) civil society as well. He took over all radio and television stations and all newspapers: Libya had no independent media. Qaddafi also published his political and social philosophy in three slim volumes that together became known as the Green Book. According to Qaddafi, the Green Book was a guide to creating the perfect society; it explained and justified his every action. It was required reading for the rest of the regime, taught in every school and displayed in every Libyan home and business.

In addition to curtailing the media and requiring the Green Book to be read, Qaddafi nationalized the banks and seized savings accounts, banned bosses, and then banned private businesses altogether. He did this in the name of "equality," but the effect on the economy was disastrous, as Libyan expatriate Guma el-Gamaty explains:

> He changed the currency just like that, said the old currency was worth nothing . . . so suddenly those people with tens of thousands of Libyan dinars in their house, it became worthless.... Then he started a rule that you were only allowed to own one house, and people were stripped of property. His own people, they started grabbing villas and houses and just living in them. He nationalized all the shops and businesses and companies. Even corner shops were closed down.
>
> ... Even toothpaste was not available.... People reverted to the old days of cleaning teeth with charcoal.[23]

Creating a Cult of Personality

Qaddafi did everything he could to cultivate an image of himself as Libya's all-powerful savior and protector, browbeating Libyans with his message and saturating the country with his image. His vanity, it seemed, was unlimited.

He created a government archive of his every speech and written document and broadcast daily readings of the Green Book on TV. Garish images of Qaddafi were literally everywhere: on walls of buildings and rugs on the floor, on lamp posts, on billboards lining every road, even in the middle of the desert. His face, with its unsmiling gaze, hardly aged over the decades. Irish national Michael Cullen, who arrived in Libya in the 1980s to work as a construction supervisor, recalls: "There were huge billboards of Ghaddafi on the approach to Benghazi as well as in the airport. Full-size likenesses in all his finery, both in his Arab garb as well as his military uniform. The famous photo of Ghaddafi standing at the helm of the motorboat with sword raised in anger against the foreign military ships was also displayed at the airport."[24]

Qaddafi worked hard to personify and cultivate an image of himself as an all-powerful savior and protector.

Stifling Dissent

At the same time that Qaddafi set out to make Libyans revere him, he took extreme measures to quash opposition to his regime. Strikes and demonstrations of any kind were banned.

Organizations—for example, associations of doctors or hobbyist clubs—were allowed to exist but had no real function because meetings of all kinds were banned. In Qaddafi's increasingly paranoid view, meetings might lead to opposition. Even sports teams were banned as potentially subversive.

Qaddafi removed anyone suspected of disloyalty from civilian and military posts. He filled those positions with fellow Qaddafa tribesmen, true believers in his cult of personality, paid political loyalists, and close family members.

Libyans' Standard of Living Improves

Qaddafi did enact some measures that improved his people's standard of living—up to a point. For example, he instituted universal free education from elementary school through university.

Many Libyans participated in a Muammar Qaddafi parade where citizens demonstrated their support of the Libyan leader. During his time in power, Qaddafi enacted some measures that increased the Libyan people's standard of living.

Qaddafi's Amazonian Guard

One of Qaddafi's most bizarre creations was his elite team of female bodyguards, dubbed by Western journalists the Amazonian Guard. Beginning in the 1980s, Qaddafi kept a unit of about thirty hand-picked, uniformed women at his side. Qaddafi himself maintained that the all-female unit was part of his philosophy of equality of the sexes. Skeptical observers suggested it was either a security tactic—Qaddafi figuring that would-be assassins would be reluctant to shoot at women—or a reflection of the dictator's vanity to surround himself with attractive women.

Candidates for the Amazonian Guard had to be tall, beautiful, and have long hair. Some four hundred were chosen over the years. They underwent intensive training in weaponry and martial arts and were dressed in an odd mixture of military fatigues with designer desert boots and Western hairstyles, high heels, and nail polish.

Though they appeared glamorous, Qaddafi's elite female guards did not lead glamorous lives. Housed in cramped barracks, they were required to take vows of chastity but were reportedly raped by Qaddafi's men and even family members. Nineteen-year-old guard Nisrine Abdul Hadi told reporters, "We had three jobs. To support the male army, to do ceremonial things—like guarding. And to fight if necessary." In the 2011 uprising that brought down Qaddafi, fighting was necessary: Several Amazonian Guards told reporters they were ordered to shoot rebel prisoners or be killed themselves.

Quoted in Martin Chulov. "Gaddafi's Amazonian Bodyguards Barracks Quashes Myth of Glamour." *Guardian* (Manchester, UK), September 7, 2011. www.guardian.co.uk/world/2011/sep/07/gaddafis-amazonian-bodyguards-barracks.

This led to a jump in the literacy rate from 40 percent in 1973 to 82.6 percent in 2011. Qaddafi himself designed the educational curricula, however, and clamped down on teachers who strayed from his teaching materials or methods.

He also provided free health care for all Libyans. Hospital quality, however, was poor compared with the other oil-rich Arab states, such as Kuwait or the United Arab Emirates. Standards of medical care in general were low.

In some ways, women were less restricted in Qaddafi's Libya than in other Muslim countries. With Qaddafi's approval, many Libyan women chose not to cover their faces with the Muslim veil, and large numbers entered the workforce in the 1970s. Their occupations, however, were mostly limited to teaching or secretarial jobs, and in the Green Book Qaddafi calls women "the feebler sex."[25]

Policies Go Awry

Part of Qaddafi's grand plan for democracy was compulsory military training for both young men and women. This policy upset most Libyans, who traditionally thought it was inappropriate for women to serve in the military. Qaddafi prevailed; he opened the Women's Academy to train women soldiers, seven thousand of whom graduated in 1983. Popular disapproval was so strong, however, that eventually Qaddafi quietly ended the policy and closed the school.

Many of Qaddafi's economic policies also backfired; for example, he provided cheap food staples, such as rice and flour, but Libyans could only buy these goods in state-run markets, where the range and supply of goods was always unpredictable.

Another economic policy meant to foster equality was that Libyans were guaranteed monthly stipends, or cash payments, that enabled most people to own a house and a car. Under Qaddafi, annual per capita income rose from ten thousand to twelve thousand dollars. This was five times that of Egyptians but low compared with other oil-rich nations. Moreover, Libyans' buying power slowly eroded because the government wage he set in the early 1970s was frozen at the same amount for nearly twenty years. Most unwisely, Qaddafi failed to use oil wealth to develop Libya into a modern state like Dubai or Qatar. With no private industry allowed, unemployment rose to more than 30 percent.

The Green Book

Sometimes described as a how-to manual for dictators, Qaddafi's Green Book is full of contradictory instructions for achieving pure democracy by doing away with democratic processes such as elections. It is also full of silly or nonsensical statements presented as if they were the profound insights of a great thinker. Here are a few of the lessons that generations of Libyan schoolchildren were forced to memorize:

Muammar Qaddafi's Green Book contains Qaddafi's contradictory and often nonsensical revolutionary theories.

It is an undisputed fact that both man and woman are human beings.... Women are different from men in form because they are females.

If a community of people wears white on a mournful occasion and another dresses in black, then one community would like white and dislike black and the other would like black and dislike white.... This attitude leaves a physical effect on the cells as well as on the genes in the body.

Sporting clubs which constitute the traditional sports institutions in the world today are rapacious social instruments. The grandstands of public athletic fields are actually constructed to block access to the fields.

Quoted in Andrew Roberts. "The Top 10 Quotes from Gaddafi's Green Book." *Daily Beast,* March 2, 2011. www.thedailybeast.com/articles/2011/03/02/gaddafis-green-book-the-top-10-quotes.html.

Meanwhile, Qaddafi used Libya's treasury (99 percent of which came from oil revenues) as his personal bank. In addition to paying off layers of military and police units for protection and loyalty, he funded building and infrastructure projects that improved roads and drew many rural Libyans to the cities to live. Spending was mostly concentrated in the Tripoli area, however, and the coastal region as far east as his home town of Sirte. Benghazi, far to the east and the stronghold of the deposed King Idris and his tribe, was left on its own. Over time, neglect led to the deterioration of Benghazi and living conditions in the entire eastern region.

The Great Man-Made River

Qaddafi's most ambitious infrastructure project was funding a huge irrigation network he called the Great Man-Made River (and, sometimes, the Eighth Wonder of the World). Its purpose was

The opening of the Great Man-Made River occurred in 1991. It brings water from southern Libyan subterranean aquifers to the coastal north and is sometimes referred to as the Eighth Wonder of the World.

to pump freshwater from a vast underground aquifer in Libya's southern desert. More than thirteen hundred wells would bring some of the water to the surface to irrigate new agriculture projects. A gigantic network of underground pipes would channel most of the water to Tripoli, Benghazi, Sirte, and other population centers.

With Qaddafi's full support, the design and plans for the Great Man-Made River took shape in the early 1970s. Construction of the mammoth project proceeded in stages, beginning in 1984, and continues to the present day. When completed, the project is predicted to supply Libya with enough freshwater to last a thousand years.

Libya Gets a New Name

By the end of the 1970s, Qaddafi's Libya was a closed society and Qaddafi its undisputed dictator. From then on, the message the outside world received was that Qaddafi was an enlightened ruler beloved by his people. Inside Libya, however, two generations of Libyans would grow up amid repression and fear. Knowing nothing else *but* Qaddafi, Libyans settled for the limited social benefits he offered them and kept their criticisms to themselves.

Qaddafi claimed he had no official role in governing the country, that he lived on a modest salary, and that the state's only function was to hand out oil revenues. As if to prove that, in 1977 he renamed the country the People's Socialist Libyan Arab Jamahiriyya (the latter his word for "statelessness") and declared that Libya was the only perfect democracy in the world. Claiming to have accomplished his revolution inside the country, he set out to spread revolution around the world. His unprincipled drive to become a major player in international politics would soon make him an international villain.

Chapter 4

Rogue Leader of a Rogue Nation

By the end of the 1970s, Qaddafi's grand plans for a pan-Arab state had gone nowhere. Taking no responsibility, Qaddafi blamed the Libyan people for lack of commitment to his revolution and other Arab leaders for not bowing to his leadership. He thus embarked on twenty years of conflict and bloodshed. This included crackdowns on his own people and terrorist acts—which he called revolutionary movements—outside of Libya. The alienated and outraged international community responded by imposing harsh sanctions on Libya, which increased Libyans' misery but did little to change the dictator's ways.

Going After Opponents Inside Libya

In the upheaval of Qaddafi's 1970s reforms, educated moderates who wanted to make Libya a modern, stable, functioning state tried in vain to present their ideas. Qaddafi's increasingly paranoid response was to tighten control over all aspects of Libyan society. Shortly after his so-called five points address, he canceled all school vacations and forced students to attend what he called a summer cultural school. This featured nonstop, heavy-handed revolutionary and religious teachings designed to prevent students from thinking for themselves.

As early as 1974, Qaddafi had warned his people they would be punished if they tried to organize against him: "I could at any moment send them to the People's Court ... and the People's

A giant poster of Libyan President Muammar Qaddafi is shown hanging in Tripoli's central Green Square. Qaddafi, paranoid by new ideas that went against his own reforms, took many measures to tighten control over his people.

Court will issue a sentence of death, because execution is the fate of anyone who forms a political party."[26] And he backed up his threats: Arrests, imprisonment without trial, torture, and public executions began immediately. Hangings and mutilations were broadcast on state television. In one notorious example, Qaddafi personally oversaw the 1984 public hanging of two students from Tripoli University accused of being involved in protest activities.

Perhaps the worst of Qaddafi's repressive measures was the Law of Collective Punishment. This law authorized the state—that is, Qaddafi—to punish entire families or towns for the actions of individuals. "Collective punishment will be carried out on a community even when the identity of the person(s) concerned has not been established," reported the human rights watchdog organization Amnesty International in 1997. "In practice, families of suspected government opponents have long been subjected to various forms of punishment, including being held as hostages. House destruction is another form of collective punishment and several prominent Libyan figures in exile have had their properties, including houses, destroyed."[27]

Going After Opponents Outside Libya

The enemy Qaddafi hated and feared most was a Libyan opposition movement working to depose him from outside the country. The core of this opposition movement were Libyans who had been sent abroad by Qaddafi to study at Western universities and return with needed technical skills. Once they experienced life in free societies, however, many chose not to return home. From a distance, these exiles dared to criticize Qaddafi and his abuses of power. An outraged Qaddafi labeled them "stray dogs" who were "worthy of slaughter."[28]

In 1980 Qaddafi began sending death squads abroad to kill the dissidents on the streets of Western cities. One of these cities was Boulder, Colorado, home to the University of Colorado.

"In 1980, while the Libyan government still maintained an embassy in Washington, a Libyan agent attempted to assassinate dissident Faisal Zagallai, a doctoral student at the University of Colorado, Boulder," writes Mohamed Eljahmi of the American Libyan Freedom Alliance in the *Middle East Quarterly.* "The bullets left Zagallai partially blinded."[29]

In another incident, on April 17, 1984, dissidents calling themselves the National Front for the Salvation of Libya staged a peaceful protest at the Libyan embassy in London (renamed the London People's Bureau by Qaddafi, who thought that sounded more revolutionary). Qaddafi's men inside the embassy opened machine-gun fire on the crowd, injuring eleven protesters and killing a twenty-five-year-old British policewoman. Britain broke off relations with Libya over the incident and kicked the Libyan diplomats out of the country.

Courting the Soviet Union

By then, U.S.-Libyan relations had already broken down. Qaddafi's anti-American speech had incited a Libyan mob to attack and set fire to the American embassy in Tripoli in December 1979. That incident prompted Washington to withdraw American diplomats from Libya in February 1980. Within a year, American officials had expelled Libyan diplomats from Washington, D.C., after Qaddafi's "stray dogs" campaign came to light.

American officials did not much like Libyan diplomats anyway, because Qaddafi was quite cozy with the Soviet Union, America's enemy during the Cold War. During this decades-long conflict, the two superpowers vied for power and influence around the globe. Qaddafi sought to unnerve the United States by cozying up to the Soviet Union. In 1975 he had announced a deal with the Soviets to build Libya's first nuclear reactor. The prospect of a pro-Soviet Qaddafi in control of nuclear weapons set off alarms in Washington. Qaddafi seemed to enjoy rankling the Americans by state visits to Moscow and all-smiles pictures with Soviet premier Leonid Brezhnev. In one interview, Qaddafi needled the United States in his usual partly joking,

Muammar Qaddafi (seated right) meeting with Cuba's Fidel Castro in 1977. In order to unnerve the United States, Qaddafi went out of his way to cozy up to Communist, pro-Soviet countries, like Cuba.

partly threatening style: " I am not a communist, but I might be obliged—just to nag America—to become a communist out of spite."[30]

In addition to the nuclear reactor deal, Qaddafi bought billions of dollars of weapons and equipment from the Soviet Union and hired experts from other Communist, pro-Soviet countries; for example, Cuban military advisers, East German intelligence agents, and North Korean pilots.

Trouble with Countries Closer to Home

In addition to alienating the United States and Britain, Qaddafi managed to make enemies of two of Libya's neighbors during the late 1970s and 1980s. First, Libya and Egypt had a series of gun battles in a short border war in 1977 that ended with a tense cease-fire. A much longer, bloodier, and costlier conflict began in 1978 when Qaddafi went to war with Libya's southern neighbor, Chad.

The dispute was over a rectangular, nearly empty 44,000-square-mile (113, 960 sq. km) piece of the Sahara Desert along the border of the two countries known as the Aouzou Strip. Qaddafi claimed it as Libyan territory. A series of offensives, occupations, and retreats prolonged the conflict until 1987. Though a diplomatic settlement was eventually reached, after which relations between Libya and Chad slowly improved, the war left Qaddafi with a lasting hatred of France, which had supported Chad in the war.

Support for Terrorism

The violence Qaddafi is best known for, however, was not conventional war but support for and sponsorship of international terrorism. Always careful to avoid evidence of his direct involvement, his support for a series of attacks in the 1970s–1990s is not in doubt.

Qaddafi was first associated with terrorism in September 1972, when Israeli athletes were murdered during the Summer Olympic Games held in Munich, Germany. Eight terrorists from the Palestinian paramilitary group Black September snuck into the Olympic Village and took eleven members and officials of the Israeli wrestling team hostage. A horrified international audience watched events unfold on television: As the terrorists attempted to escape with the hostages, German police launched a failed rescue. In the gun battle that followed, five terrorists were killed and three were captured, but not before they had killed all of the Israelis.

The memorial service for the eleven victims of the Munich massacre was held at the Munich Olympic Stadium. The massacre was Qaddafi's first association with terrorism.

Training Camps for Terrorism

In *Terrorism: The Soviet Connection* (1984), circulated by the U.S. State Department in 1986, authors Ray S. Cline and Yonah Alexander cited *Akher Sa'a*, an Egyptian weekly newsmagazine, in identifying ten major terrorist training camps run by Qaddafi with Soviet assistance inside Libya:

1. Al-'Azizyya Camp (south of Tripoli): training the Polisario Front and international terrorists
2. Al-Ma'had Camp (the name means "the institute"): training Libyan terrorists
3. Al-Sa'iqa Camp (no location given; the name means "lightning bolt"): training Africans, Palestinians, Italian Red Brigades, and members of the Basque Separatists
4. Al-Shahid Maqarief Camp: training Libyans
5. Sebha Camp West: training terrorists
6. Jaghbub Camp (at the Jaghbub or Jarabub Oasis, near Egypt): training extremist groups
7. Surt Camp (at Surt or Sirte on the Gulf of Sirte): training assassins
8. Tarahuna Camp (southeast of Tripoli): training extremist Arab groups
9. Taybmi Camp: training extremist Tunisian groups
10. Umm al-Aranib Camp (about 25 miles south of Sebha Oasis): training assassins

Quoted in Christian Gomez. "Gadhafi's Libya, Agent of the Soviet Menace." *New American*, February 23, 2011. http://thenewamerican.com/world-mainmenu-26/africa-mainmenu-27/6439-gadhafis-libya-agent-of-the-soviet-menace.

Qaddafi had not planned or funded the Munich massacre. He did, however, celebrate the Black September perpetrators, both living and dead. The bodies of the five terrorists killed were delivered to Libya, where Qaddafi honored them with a burial with full military honors. Less than two months later, the three captured Black Septemberists were released as part of a separate airline hijacking deal and flown to Libya, where Qaddafi and cheering crowds give them a hero's welcome.

The first terrorist attack linked to Qaddafi occurred on December 17, 1973. Palestinian terrorists, who claimed to be acting on direct orders from Qaddafi, massacred more than thirty people at the Rome airport and hijacked a German airliner. The hijackers were turned over to Palestine Liberation Organization (PLO) officials as part of an Egypt-brokered deal, and the Qaddafi link was never proven.

This terrorist act would not be Qaddafi's last. Pursuing his goal of Libyan-style revolution abroad, Qaddafi funneled money and explosives to many different terrorists and terrorist groups, including the Irish Republican Army; the Venezuelan-born Carlos the Jackal; Abu Nidal, the Palestinian founder of the militant Fatah movement; and into the 1990s, Osama bin Laden's al Qaeda organization.

Qaddafi Versus Reagan

Qaddafi's support for terrorism gave him the spotlight he wanted. *Newsweek* magazine titled a dramatic July 1981 cover story, "Kaddafi: The Most Dangerous Man in the World?"[31] Although urged to tone down his demonization, which advisers said only gave Qaddafi more influence, U.S. president Ronald Reagan publicly called him the "mad dog of the Middle East," "Gaddafi Duck," "a flake," and "a barbarian."[32]

Indeed, the two men loathed each other: Qaddafi was rumored to have plotted an attempted assassination of Reagan in 1981. Qaddafi denied any such thing in an ABC interview in December 1981. By then, however, U.S.-Libya relations were in tatters. Along with breaking off diplomatic relations, Reagan imposed a Libyan oil embargo in 1981. Before the embargo, the United States was buying 40 percent of Libyan oil exports, which equaled 10 percent of U.S. oil consumption. By 1985, economic sanctions banned the shipment of all products to Libya except medicines and food. They also froze Libyan assets in U.S. banks. Americans working in Libya were ordered to return home, and lots of foreign aid was given to African countries willing to oppose Qaddafi.

The Bombing of Tripoli

Europeans were not as vehemently opposed to Qaddafi as the United States was. For one thing, European governments bought a lot of Libyan oil and had many workers stationed in Libya. They also realized that in an all-out war, Europe was a lot closer to Libya geographically, and thus a much closer target of Libyan military attacks, than was the United States. In general, Europeans suggested that Reagan was overreacting to Qaddafi and exaggerating the threat he posed.

A street scene showing the aftermath of a bomb exploding in a crowded West Berlin nightclub, Las Belle Discotheque, on April 5, 1986. Qaddafi was the suspected mastermind behind the attack, which prompted retaliation by the United States.

Did Hana Die?

In retaliation for the West Berlin nightclub bombing, President Ronald Reagan ordered air strikes against Tripoli and Benghazi in 1986. Qaddafi and other members of his family claimed that his daughter Hana was killed during these strikes, but this story has been disputed.

In 2011, a passport, photographs, and other documents identifying Hana Qaddafi as a medical school graduate working in Tripoli were discovered in the Qaddafi family home. Qaddafi family sources claim this young woman is a second adopted daughter named in honor of the dead Hana. Many Libyans, however, have argued for years that Hana Qaddafi survived the bombing and that the dictator's story was propaganda invented to stir up anti-American sentiment.

Then, on April 5, 1986, a bomb exploded in a crowded West Berlin nightclub, La Belle Discotheque, popular with U.S. service members. Three people were killed and some 230, including nearly 80 U.S. soldiers, were injured. Communications between the Libyan embassy in East Berlin and Tripoli at the time of the bombing, intercepted by Americans, said a successful operation had taken place that could not be traced to Libya.

Ten days later, in a controversial move, Reagan ordered air strikes against Tripoli and Benghazi in Operation El Dorado Canyon. The targets of the retaliation were a suspected intelligence/terrorism headquarters, military bases and airfields, and the Bab el-Aziziyya Barracks in Tripoli where Qaddafi and his family lived. Son Saif al-Islam gives his version of the event:

I was only fourteen at the time and my family were all together in our home in Tripoli. One night, without any warning, the bombers came and, for five minutes, rained rockets down on us. I was woken up by loud crashing sounds and explosions, it was absolutely terrifying.... Some of my brothers and sisters were too young to know what to do, and they became trapped in one part of the house when a corridor collapsed.... When we dug them out we found that Hana, my youngest sister, had died. She was just four years old.[33]

In a national televised address two hours after the bombing, Reagan told the American people that "today we have done what we had to do. If necessary, we shall do it again."[34]

The attack may have made Qaddafi look vulnerable, but his survival, and the fact that no one tried to overthrow him in the aftermath, seemed to enhance his status. To Qaddafi and his supporters, the attack proved he was important enough to be a superpower's major enemy and that he had stood up to American aggression.

Lockerbie

The event that branded Qaddafi as a villain and a madman around the world was the bombing of an international Pan American Airlines flight on December 21, 1988. At the time, the bombing was the most deadly terrorist attack on civilians in history. On December 21, Pan Am Flight 103 from London to New York exploded in midair over Lockerbie, Scotland, killing all 259 people aboard the airplane and 11 people on the ground.

Western intelligence agencies had been on alert for a possible terrorist attack, and several terrorist groups claimed responsibility. After a three-year investigation, two Libyan nationals were accused of planting the bomb. Warrants for their arrest were issued, but Qaddafi refused to hand them over to European officials for trial.

Shocked and horrified by the disaster, the leaders of major industrialized nations vowed to fight terrorism and singled out Qaddafi as a major perpetrator. The United States and the United Nations imposed harsh sanctions on Libya, cutting supplies of all but humanitarian aid. They banned Libyan imports and travel to Libya, and froze Qaddafi's foreign bank accounts. U.S. oil companies left Libya.

Arab leaders offered Qaddafi weak verbal support but kept their distance from the increasingly isolated dictator. Europeans went relatively easy on him: From 1991 to 2004, 85 percent of Libyan exports went to Europe, and Libya was Germany and Italy's biggest source of oil. The deprivation inside Libya, however, was severe. Hardest hit were the east (including Benghazi) and the south, as Qaddafi doled out little money in those areas.

Qaddafi, International Pariah

The 1990s was a decade of near-total exclusion of Libya from world affairs. Isolated and repressed, Libyans were dominated in all ways of life by Qaddafi. Their plight rarely reached the outside world, however, because travel to Libya was strictly limited and news from inside the country strictly censored.

Qaddafi the Megalomaniac

By the late 1970s, Qaddafi was exhibiting signs of megalomania, which is a mental defect characterized by an irrational belief in one's own importance and power. His egotism was unlimited. In 1976, for example, he had his court musician write a song called "Messenger of the Arabian Desert," which compared Qaddafi to the Prophet Muhammad, founder of Islam. In 1992 Qaddafi released a Libyan postage stamp that pictured himself on a winged white horse leaping into the sky, just as Muhammad was said to have ridden a winged white horse from Mecca to Jerusalem.

Qaddafi encouraged his underlings to see him as godlike: He succeeded in converting some to this belief, such as Revolutionary Guard commander Hasan al-Kabir al-Qadhafi (no relation), who said in 2005 that Qaddafi was a living saint who had a special relationship with Allah (the name for God in Islam).

In the 1990s Qaddafi dominated his people and was resented for his lavish, indulgent lifestyle.

Qaddafi seemed unperturbed and unrepentant. He lived lavishly, forced his people to listen to speeches that went on for three or four hours, and occupied himself with self-indulgent projects. In 1999, for example, he designed his own automobile, the Saroukh el-Jamahiriyya, or "Rocket of the Republic." According to Daniel Kawczynski, it was "a missile-shaped, dark green [sedan] with safety features designed by the Leader himself. A Libyan spokesman claimed that 'the invention of the safest car in the world is proof that the Libyan revolution is built on the happiness of man.' The design was updated for the fortieth anniversary celebrations [of Qaddafi's coup] in 2009, but was said to be still awaiting mass production."[35]

Not until the end of the 1990s did Qaddafi seek to rehabilitate his image. To some extent he would succeed in rejoining the international community—but more as an object of ridicule than as a world leader.

Chapter 5

Qaddafi Comes In from the Cold

In the 2000s, Qaddafi reinvented himself yet again as a statesman and a peacemaker. His flamboyance, staying power, and enormous wealth guaranteed him an audience in Africa and the West, but nowhere was he considered trustworthy. The "new" Qaddafi had two goals: to maintain his grip on Libya and to be seen as a great political thinker and statesman on the world stage.

First Signs of Change

One of the first signs that Qaddafi was willing to cooperate with, and behave sanely toward, other nations was his agreement to turn over the two Libyan nationals accused of the bombing of Pan Am 103 in 1988 to Scottish officials. In 1999 the two men were delivered to Scottish custody; the next year they stood trial in the Netherlands.

Neither man testified at his trial nor expressed remorse—or a motive—for the bombing. (Prosecutors argued that Qaddafi ordered the bombing in retaliation for skirmishes between U.S. and Libyan fighter planes over the Gulf of Sidra in the early 1980s in which a Libyan plane was shot down.) One of the defendants was acquitted, but the other was found guilty and sentenced to life in prison. At the time, Qaddafi had no comment other than to deny his involvement.

A second sign that Qaddafi was, at least publicly, ready to renounce violence was his strong condemnation of the

Qaddafi showed willingness to cooperate with other nations when he agreed to turn over two Libyan nationals accused of bombing Pan Am 103.

September 11, 2001, terrorist attacks on the United States. In these, nineteen Saudi Arabian terrorists hijacked four commercial airplanes and flew three of them into buildings in the United States, killing nearly three thousand people. The fourth was diverted from its target by passengers and crashed in a field. Even though Qaddafi expressed his sympathy for the attacks, the United States, the imposer of the harshest sanctions and the source of the strongest anti-Qaddafi sentiment, was reluctant to thaw relations. In 2002, Qaddafi agreed to set up a $2.7 billion fund for victims of the Lockerbie bombing (without admitting guilt), but still the U.S. sanctions stayed in place.

The Turning Point

The turning point came in 2003, for three reasons. First, an international military coalition led by the United States invaded Iraq and toppled its longtime dictator, Saddam Hussein. Qaddafi may have viewed the war as a sign that the U.S. would no longer tolerate defiant dictators like himself. No doubt he did not want to be the next Saddam Hussein, who was found dirty and disoriented and hiding in a hole in the ground, paraded before news cameras, and hanged as a common criminal.

Second, militant Islamist fundamentalist movements, which Qaddafi called "more dangerous than AIDS,"[36] were inciting violent uprisings across the Middle East. The Islamists were more than religious conservatives. Their goal was to create Islamic states with an Islamic government, laws, legal system, armed forces, and social codes, all according to their strict interpretation of the religion. Qaddafi, who saw Islamic militants as a serious threat to his power, decided the best way to keep his grip on Libya was to, after all these years, ally himself with Western powers.

Finally, Qaddafi needed money. The economic sanctions had taken their toll on the Libyan treasury. Libya was rich in oil reserves, but in dire need of modernization after three decades of repressive dictatorship. Qaddafi knew that would take foreign investment, which in turn required the loosening of sanctions against his regime.

Concessions, and a Wary Truce

In a major move toward restoring relations, in 2003 Qaddafi announced he was shutting down Libya's nuclear weapons program and allowing inspections of the closed facilities. Even Westerners who had been investigating Qaddafi's quest for weapons of mass destruction (WMD) for decades were surprised to learn how much he had spent on the nuclear weapons program just in the late 1990s: $500 million.

Journalist Robert Fisk, one of few foreign journalists allowed into Libya during the years Qaddafi was an international outcast, was not impressed by Qaddafi's announcement, however. Fisk doubted Qaddafi's nuclear program posed a threat in the first place. In Fisk's view, Qaddafi could barely run a country, let alone produce advanced weapons. "The problem I have with the whole Gaddafi saga," Fisk said, "is that the Libya I know can scarcely repair a drain or install a working lavatory in a hotel."[37]

Muammar Qaddafi (right) is shown shaking hands with Britain's Prime Minister Tony Blair on March 25, 2004. The Prime Minister's visit was a sign of acceptance of the reformed Qaddafi.

Just how serious a threat Qaddafi's WMD program was remains uncertain. Like much of Qaddafi's bombastic rhetoric, his claims to be building a nuclear weapon were exaggerated. Libya had not actually produced any weapons-grade plutonium, the key ingredient for a nuclear weapon. It also did not have the infrastructure or scientists required to run a successful program. Nevertheless, his intentions were serious, and his gesture did help to rehabilitate his image in the United States.

Qaddafi made other gestures intended to show he had turned over a new leaf. In 2004, for example, he cooperated with the U.S. government and worked with the Central Intelligence Agency (CIA) to find and turn over additional terrorist suspects. That same year, he set up a $35 million compensation fund for victims of the Berlin nightclub bombing.

Gradually, most of the bans on Libyan exports and imports were lifted. As Qaddafi made good on his promises to pay restitution to victims of terrorism, his foreign assets were unfrozen.

Qaddafi at the United Nations

On September 22, 2009, Qaddafi addressed the United Nations General Assembly. It was the most prestigious appearance of his life, but he did not rise to the occasion. Shaking his fist or a copy of the UN Charter, he delivered a rambling, nonstop hundred-minute harangue ranging from criticism of the UN to conspiracy theories about swine flu and the assassination of U.S. president John F. Kennedy.

The browbeating tested everyone's patience, especially the Arabic interpreters on the UN staff. "He's not exactly the most lucid speaker," said one. "It's not just that what he's saying is illogical, but the way he's saying it is bizarre.... Khadafy has a habit of repeating the same phrase over and over again, which is good because if you don't understand what he says the first time you can get it right the second or third time." Another added, "Sometimes he mumbles, sometimes he talks to himself."

After Qaddafi's record-breaking diatribe, the interpreters were given a day off. Said one, "Ten minutes with Khadafy earns you a lot of annual leave."

Quoted in Chuck Bennett and Jeremy Olshan. "Translator Collapsed During Kadhafi's Rambling Diatribe," *New York Post*, September 24, 2009. www.nypost.com/p/news/international/translator_collapsed_during_khadafy_EAHR9j2jHOt8Y6TFRhrcQM.

President George W. Bush issued an executive order allowing American businesses back in Libya.

As a sign of acceptance of the reformed Qaddafi, British prime minister Tony Blair made a much-publicized first visit to Qaddafi's Libya in 2004. Theatrically staged by Qaddafi in a desert-tent setting, the two leaders met with press photographers on hand to witness handshakes and a new spirit of cooperation. Qaddafi ventured beyond Libya, too, traveling to a European Union meeting in Brussels in 2004, his first trip outside Africa or the Middle East in fifteen years.

Good-bye Arab World, Hello Africa

The Arab world was not much interested in punishing Libya anymore, either. Most Arab leaders, however, saw Qaddafi as a rival who would turn on any ally in his own self-interest, and they

From Pan-Arabism to Pan-Africanism

Qaddafi wanted to lead a pan-African United States of Africa in the 2000s, much as he once dreamed of leading a pan-Arab state. In his 2005 book *My Vision,* Qaddafi gave journalist Edmond Jouve typically odd, nonsensical answers about his new aim and the conflicting news that he was also, at the same time, expelling black Africans from Libya:

Gaddafi: Libya is now a member of the African Union. From now on there is no room for Nationalism and ethnic claims. International communities based on regions and continents are more appropriate in our age. As a result, two-tier politics is no longer possible. Libya belongs to the African continent and as the Africans have decided to create the United States of Africa, we cannot run two types of policy at the same time: one for the Arab League and another for the African Union. It would be too difficult!

Jouve: There is the case of the black people who were expelled from Libya. What is the explanation for that? …

Gaddafi: In actual fact this problem is perfectly comprehensible. It was not surprising that it should arise at the time when the African Union process was underway particularly between the inhabitants of North Africa, who are white, and those of sub-Saharan Africa, who are black. In most cases, it is a question of personalities.

Muammar Gaddafi with Edmond Jouve. *My Vision.* London: John Blake, 2005, pp. 83, 86.

kept their distance. Shunned by the Arab world but seeking, as always, a role to match his ego, Qaddafi turned instead to making plays for power in Africa.

Envisioning himself as a peacemaker now, he invited Sudanese officials to Tripoli for cease-fire talks to help solve the bloody civil war there. He also funded medical and refugee missions to Darfur, the region in Sudan hit hardest by the civil war.

Just as he had once ordered his people to think of themselves as Arabs rather than Libyans, he now ordered them to think of themselves as Africans, with a shared history and destiny. He promoted a new political union: the United States of Africa, with a single currency he called the *afro* and himself as president. No such thing happened, but he did manage to establish (and head) a loose political alliance of fifty-four African countries called the African Union in 2002.

In Qaddafi's new vision, he would be revered as the African king of kings. All over the country, images of his face on giant billboards were now accompanied by adoring quotations on walls and arches painted in the bright green of Qaddafi's Libyan flag: With him we live, without him we die," "Falcon of Africa— Thinker and Leader," "To you alone, O Leader, love and adoration," "The Liberator—Dawn of Freedom."[38]

A Traumatized Nation

Infatuated with his new dream of becoming the African king of kings, Qaddafi spent little time repairing the damage a decade of harsh sanctions had wrought on his country. He paid little attention to the Libyan people beyond maintaining his spy networks and police activities. As an example of Qaddafi's repression, by 2005 Libya was a country with ten universities but more than 120 prisons.

The years of deprivation and fear had taken their toll on ordinary Libyans. Arrest, interrogation, torture, and imprisonment (and the ultimate punishments, "disappearance" and execution) awaited anyone suspected of insufficient loyalty to Qaddafi or commitment to the revolution. That included, for example, listening to religious tapes from non-Libyan sources or belonging

A billboard in Libya displays an image of Qaddafi as the powerful, ever-watchful, Libyan leader.

to a stamp-collecting club. Even defacing a poster of Qaddafi was grounds for execution.

In writer Krista Bremer's account of her 2005 visit to Libya to meet her in-laws, she states that to enter Qaddafi's Libya is to "step inside the ransacked home of an abuser, where suffering is written on the faces of everyone you see and everything shows signs of neglect." Upon leaving the airplane and entering the airport, she was greeted by a mammoth portrait of Qaddafi. Her husband translated the Arabic inscription beneath the portrait: "Brother Qaddafi, Our souls belong to you."[39]

Back in the Political Fold

Announcing in 2008 that "there will be no more wars, raids, or acts of terrorism,"[40] Qaddafi began to meet with heads of state all over Europe. In 2009, with diplomatic relations formally reestablished, the United States posted an ambassador in Tripoli for the first time in thirty-six years.

The attitude of most countries toward Qaddafi seemed to be, "we may not like him, but we have to deal with him." Italy, on the other hand, welcomed Qaddafi with open arms. The dictator made eleven state visits to Libya's former colonial ruler in the late 2000s, where he was paraded as a guest of honor by Italy's prime minister, Silvio Berlusconi, who went so far as to kiss Qaddafi's hand. Berlusconi had many reasons for at least pretending to be Qaddafi's great friend. Italy depended on Libya for a third of its oil—in fact, the longest pipeline in the Mediterranean Sea runs directly north from the Libyan coast to the island of Sicily. Libya also owned a large chunk of the Italian stock market and paid Italian construction firms huge sums for Libyan building projects.

Although in some ways reformed, Qaddafi was still out of touch with political realities. In a January 2009 *New York Times* editorial, for example, he seemed to think Israel would forget this sponsor of Palestinian terrorism who had been calling for Israel's destruction for forty years when he called for a "just and lasting peace between Israel and the Palestinians" and said "the Jewish people want and deserve their homeland."[41] Other implausible ideas caused him to be viewed as just plain crazy. For example, he called for Israel to be replaced with a new Israeli-Palestinian state called Isratine. On another occasion he urged Jews to move to Libya and bring their skills and investment with them.

Another bizarre foreign policy suggestion came in 2009, when he submitted a proposal to the United Nations that Switzerland be abolished. Qaddafi proposed that Switzerland's German-speaking region be given to Germany, its French-speaking region to France, and its Italian-speaking region to Italy. Qaddafi's idea that Switzerland be "carved up like a wheel of Swiss cheese"[42] did not sit well with analysts, heads of state, nor the Swiss.

Living Up to His Reputation

Still, taking a chance that the new-and-improved dictator would behave himself, the United Nations allowed Qaddafi to address the General Assembly in New York City in September 2009. Allotted the same fifteen-minute speaking time given to any visiting head of state, Qaddafi took the stage, refused to give up

Qaddafi addresses the General Assembly in New York City on September 23, 2009. Going well over his allotted fifteen-minutes, Qaddafi delivered a bizarre, illogical speech, which lasted over an hour and a half.

the microphone, and launched into a hundred-minute, illogical, mumbling diatribe that left the UN secretary-general with his head in his hands. "Gaddafi fully lived up to his reputation for eccentricity, bloody-mindedness and extreme verbiage," wrote Ed Pilkington of Britain's *Guardian* newspaper, who reported that Qaddafi

> tore up a copy of the UN charter in front of startled delegates, accused the security council of being an al-Qaida like terrorist body, called for [U.S. president] George [W.] Bush and [British prime minister] Tony Blair to be put on trial for the Iraq war, demanded $7.7tn [trillion] in compensation for the ravages of colonialism on Africa, and wondered whether swine flu was a biological weapon created in a military laboratory. At one point, he even demanded to know who was behind the killing of JFK [former U.S. president John F. Kennedy].[43]

Qaddafi's own Arabic translator gave up after little more than an hour, shouting into his live microphone, "I just can't take it anymore."[44]

Weirdness on Display

Qaddafi's personal vanity and eccentricity were on display wherever he went. He appeared in public in heavy make-up and special shoes to increase his height. His outfits and uniforms, always strange, became bizarre costumes that had nothing to do with Libyan traditions. According to Qaddafi biographer Daniel Kawczynski, foreign leaders tended to stand as far away from the dictator as possible, with expressions of obvious distaste, when he attended meetings in clownish outfits. Kawczynski chronicles just a few of these outfits, which included "a blinding white suit covered by an Arab *bisht* for the 2009 G8 [economic] summit, an aviation-themed leather and fur ensemble for a visit to Versailles [the former French royal palace, now a museum] in 2007, a long shirt emblazoned with photographs of African heroes to see President [Hosni] Mubarak of Egypt in August 2005, flowing peach and purple silk robes to meet the Portuguese prime minister, Antonio Guterres, in April 2000."[45]

Qaddafi's living arrangements on his various state visits were just as bizarre. He insisted that he be allowed to set up and conduct meetings from a huge, heated (and bulletproof) Bedouin tent flown in at great expense along with an entourage of as many as four hundred people. Camels were sometimes part of that entourage.

Foreign interviewers found Qaddafi increasingly vague. As historian Dirk Vandewalle reports, "He had this habit of kind of staring off into space all the time. And there were long pauses in which you didn't know if he had really understood you.... But then usually the answer that you would get was a very kind of pedestrian answer, or he would simply refer you to the 'Green Book.' So there wasn't much of a substance there."[46]

Qaddafi's enjoyment of the limelight would be short-lived. Imagining himself beloved and invincible, mistaking celebrity for respect, he was perhaps the only one surprised to find his regime come crashing down in 2011.

Chapter 6

The Bloody End of a Tyrant

After forty-two years in power, after all the intrigue and effort he expended to keep himself in power, Qaddafi's fall was quick and merciless. As political journalist Jon Lee Anderson writes, the Libyan tyrant's downfall followed the pattern of so many vain dictators who eventually meet their humiliating end:

> How does it end? [A] dictator dies, shrivelled and demented, in his bed; he flees the rebels in a private plane; he is caught hiding in a mountain outpost, a drainage pipe, a spider hole. He is tried. He is not tried. He is dragged, bloody and dazed, through the streets, then executed. The humbling comes in myriad forms, but what is revealed is always the same: the technologies of paranoia, the stories of slaughter and fear, the vaults, the national economies employed as personal property, the crazy pets, ... the golden fixtures. [47]

The Arab Spring: The Revolution Begins

In the spring of 2011, democracy movements flared into mass protests against repressive regimes all over the Middle East and North Africa. Tunisia's dictator, Zine el Abidine Ben Ali, fled the country on January 15. Weeks later Hosni Mubarak stepped down in Egypt after thirty years of one-man rule.

Revolutionary fighters are shown holding a pre-Qaddafi era national flag. Most of the rebels fighting against the Qaddafi regime consisted of young, male, untrained civilians.

Emboldened by what they saw happening all around them, on February 15–16 rioters in Benghazi protested the arrest of Fethi Tarbel, a human rights activist who had campaigned for the release of political prisoners. More riots broke out. By February 24, Benghazi was in opposition control, and uprisings were breaking out in coastal cities as far west as Misrata. From the capital, Qaddafi ordered a violent crackdown, including shooting unarmed protesters. Despite his attempt to quash it, the insurrection spread.

Just who was joining the rebellion was not clear. Qaddafi called the rebels Islamists, but the eastern fighters seemed to be mostly hastily assembled militias of untrained civilians who were mostly young and mostly male. They were joined by Libyan army defectors, and there was little evidence that any were religious extremists or foreign terrorists. Their weaponry and tactics were far inferior to those of Qaddafi's forces, though as the rebellion spread to the west, better-organized rebel groups raided abandoned army posts for supplies, and defectors brought their weapons with them. The leaders of the rebellion were lawyers, judges,

Qaddafi's Lifestyle Revealed

Journalist Jon Lee Anderson describes what he found when he entered Qaddafi family homes in Tripoli after victorious rebels took over the capital in September 2011.

Bab al-Aziziya . . . was not the kind of presidential residence that gives tours to schoolkids. Concrete blast walls, gun slits, and guard turrets sealed off Qaddafi and his inner circle from life in the capital. Inside the walls was a sprawling complex of intersecting compounds.... [In one area were] several of Qaddafi's elaborate tents—equipped with air-conditioning units, chandeliers, and green carpets—where he had held meetings with heads of state.... Everywhere, littering the ground, lay bits of festive-looking silver cardboard: discarded ammunition boxes for Beretta pistols.

Pathways led through gardens to an artificial hillock, where a disk-shaped house—Qaddafi's residence—was built down into the earth, like a half-buried UFO.... Many [Libyans] had believed Qaddafi's longstanding claims of a modest salary and an austere Bedouin lifestyle. Instead, they saw a private gym, an indoor swimming pool, a hairdressing salon....

Qaddafi's children owned urban villas, beach houses, and countryside retreats [with] state-of-the-art gyms, Jacuzzis, exotic cars, private zoos.... Aisha's house in Tripoli had a love seat set into a gilded sculpture of a mermaid. ... [Saif's] house had cages for his pet white tigers....

[Saadi's mansion] was set in about ten acres of olive and orange groves, surrounded by sliding stone walls on electronic tracks, which allowed the house to be shut up like a fortress. The main house was arrayed in a V around a vast swimming pool with a central island attached to the house by a hydraulic drawbridge.... A Libyan man, also touring the property, remarked with disgust, "So this was owned by a man on a four-hundred-and-seventy-five-dinar salary."

Jon Lee Anderson, "King of Kings," *New Yorker*, November 7, 2011, pp. 46, 54.

and other educated men desperate for justice, accountability, and a modern state. By late February, these leaders in Benghazi were calling themselves the Libyan National Council, later the National Transitional (or Interim) Council (NTC).

Social media sites such as Twitter played an important role in the rapid spread of the uprising. Through the Internet and smuggled cell phones, Libyans reported to and received news from the outside world, countered state propaganda, and coordinated their movements. The NTC even created its own website to spread its message.

International Economic and Political Responses

When news of Libyan army troops firing on protesters reached the outside world, the UN Security Council condemned Qaddafi for brutality against the Libyan people. They referred his actions to the International Criminal Court. The European Union imposed familiar sanctions on Qaddafi: an arms embargo, travel bans, freezing of foreign assets. Foreign companies suspended oil production on the Libyan oilfields.

On March 10, France became the first nation to recognize the NTC as the sole legitimate representative of the Libyan people. One day later, Qaddafi broke off diplomatic relations with France. In addition to the military crackdown, Qaddafi tried to starve the rebellion through his control of the country's banking network; he emptied the bank accounts of anyone thought to be sympathetic to the rebels.

Qaddafi in Denial

Qaddafi was both belligerent toward and delusional about the uprising. In February, for example, he went on national television to claim that the protesters were terrorists linked to al Qaeda who were only fighting because their coffee had been spiked with hallucinogenic drugs. Defiantly, Qaddafi swore that he would never leave Libya; he vowed to fight until his last drop of blood was

Qaddafi appearing on Libya State Television as he speaks to his followers. In his speech he vowed never to leave Libya and to continue fighting until his last drop of blood was spilled.

spilled. He was filmed for that appearance wearing a long brown robe, standing in front of a building in his Tripoli compound that had been deliberately left in ruins after the 1986 U.S. bombing attack. The ruins were intended to be a reminder of American aggression. (Since then, Qaddafi had added a statue of a U.S. fighter jet being crushed by a huge hand.)

A week later Qaddafi agreed to be interviewed by ABC correspondent Christiane Amanpour, to whom he flatly insisted there were no demonstrations against him anywhere in Libya: "They love me. All my people with me, they love me.... They will die to protect me, my people."[48] He denied using force against Libyan civilians and repeated his claim that the people who had taken over Benghazi were al Qaeda operatives. He also argued that it was impossible for him to step down because he was not president or king, that Libya was ruled by the people and he was just one of the people.

As the crisis worsened, Qaddafi's ranting took a ruthless turn. He called the rebels "rats" and swore they would be "hunted down street by street, house by house, and wardrobe by wardrobe."[49] These were not empty threats; he sent troops to Benghazi with orders to enter the city and hunt down and kill civilians. There were many reports of atrocities and massacres by Qaddafi loyalists. His son Saif al-Islam periodically issued defiant claims of victory, such as announcing on French TV, "Everything will be over in 48 hours."[50]

The NTC was just as defiant. As they wrote in a statement published on their website: "We find ourselves at a turning point with only two solutions. Either we achieve freedom and race to catch up with humanity and world developments, or we are shackled and enslaved under the feet of the tyrant Muammar Gaddafi where we shall live in the midst of history.... To liberate Libya from the hands of the tyrant Muammar Gaddafi who made lawful to himself the exploitation of his people and the wealth of his country.[51]

NATO Intervention

Benghazi was controlled by rebels and protected by a huge distance from Qaddafi forces in Tripoli and the dictator's stronghold of Sirte. Misrata, on the other hand, was rebel held but in the middle of Qaddafi-controlled territory, near Sirte, and so became the target of weeks of sustained army bombing and tank attacks. When rebel forces lost ground and Qaddafi forces fought their way to the outskirts of Benghazi, the rebels issued pleas for help. "We have God on our side and a just cause, but Qaddafi has better weapons," said thirty-four-year-old fighter Sarhan Khaled, a Libyan businessman. "We'll fight either way, but we'd like the international community to stop his planes."[52]

On March 18, the UN Security Council passed Resolution 1973 to impose a no-fly zone over Libya and approve all necessary measures (meaning military action) to protect Libyan civilians from the Libyan Army. NATO (North Atlantic Treaty Organization) air strikes began the next day. Buoyed by this support, the revolutionaries vowed to "work towards liberating the remaining cities still kidnapped by the tyrant Mu'ammar Gaddafi and his gang."[53]

Without U.S. and NATO military support, however, this would have been an empty promise. Even with US and NATO backing, one analyst notes, "it took nearly six months for the full might of NATO, bombarding every Libyan tank and armored personnel carrier that moved, decimating Qaddafi's command-and-control system, and serving as the air wing of the fractious Libyan opposition, to clear the way to Tripoli."[54] One NATO missile did strike the Qaddafi compound in Tripoli on April 30, missing Qaddafi but killing his son Saif al-Arab and three grandchildren.

Qaddafi Keeps Up the Pretense of Control

Amid the bloodshed, Qaddafi tried to show that his government was still firmly in control and functioning normally. For example, he hosted visiting South African president Jacob Zuma for cease-fire discussions. A peaceful end to the crisis was unlikely, though, as the rebels' cease-fire terms hinged on Qaddafi's stepping down, a demand Qaddafi absolutely rejected. He approved a $31.4 billion budget to fund government operations through the end of 2011, and sponsored mass pro-Qaddafi demonstrations in Tripoli's Green Square. Meanwhile, multiple sources reported that mercenaries were being flown in from elsewhere in Africa to prop up Qaddafi's forces.

At the same time, key government officials were defecting to the rebels or fleeing the country. Interior minister Abdel Fatah Younes defected to become the rebels' military chief on February 22 and was killed in fighting in late July. Foreign minister Moussa Koussa fled to Britain on March 30, and top oil minister Shokri Ghanem fled to Rome on June 1.

Politically and militarily, Qaddafi could not hold on. The NTC was recognized as the legitimate government of the Libyan state (which the NTC calls simply "Libya") by Qatar on March 28, the United States on July 15, and Great Britain on July 27. U.S. secretary of state Hillary Clinton made the

As the opposition against Qaddafi's regime strengthened, Qaddafi tried to prove to the Libyan people and the rest of the world that he was still in control. He continued to make government decisions and sponsor pro-Qaddafi demonstrations in Tripoli.

announcement: "The United States views the Gadhafi regime as no longer having any legitimate authority in Libya. And so I am announcing today that, until an interim authority is in place, the United States will recognize the NTC as the legitimate governing authority in Libya, and we will deal with it on that basis."[55]

"Get Ready for the Fight"

Accordingly, Qaddafi diplomats were expelled from foreign capitals. The Arab League suspended Libya from membership. The African Union, however, did not; not so much out of loyalty to Qaddafi as because Libya was paying 15 percent of member countries' dues and most of the cost of peacekeeping missions in Darfur and Somalia.

In June, the International Criminal Court issued arrest warrants for Qaddafi, son Saif al-Islam, and intelligence chief Abdullah al-Sanusi for crimes against humanity. On August 5, son Khamis was reported killed by a NATO strike on the western town of Zlitan. Previous reports of his death had been proven wrong, but the NTC confirmed Khamis's death on September 4.

On August 16, rebel forces captured Zawiya (cutting the coastal highway to Tunisia, a key east-west supply route to Tripoli) and Garyan (cutting the main highway leading south from Tripoli). Better-organized and better-armed western rebels advanced on the capital. By telephone call to state television on August 15, Qaddafi issued a call to his followers to "get ready for the fight.... The blood of martyrs is fuel for the battlefield."[56]

The Fall of Tripoli

Tripoli fell to rebel forces on August 22. They entered the capital with scattered last-ditch resistance from tanks and snipers, coming mostly from Qaddafi's compound Bab al-Aziziyah. Cheering crowds in Green Square welcomed the rebels, who promptly renamed the place Martyrs' Square and released some fifteen thousand political prisoners rounded up by Qaddafi forces since the uprising began.

Qaddafi himself was nowhere to be found, despite two taped messages played on state television in which he told his people he was in the capital and would be "with you until the end."[57] Rumors swirled regarding his whereabouts. One said he fled the country for Algeria on August 22 with his wife, Safia; children Muhammad, Hannibal, and Aisha; and several grandchildren. In a September 1 broadcast believed to be from

Crowds of cheering people celebrate the fall of Tripoli, which was viewed by many as the destruction of the Qaddafi regime's last remaining power in Libya.

Sirte, however, Qaddafi called on followers to keep fighting and said he would never give up. He also declared Sirte the new capital of Libya.

Family Loyalty

Public hatred and anger toward Qaddafi grew when photographs were released of his abandoned Tripoli compound. The images showed room after room stuffed with luxury goods and gaudy decor. Qaddafi's elaborate possessions included golden guns, a flyswatter made from peacock feathers, doormats with the leader's face on them, and a golden couch fashioned like a mermaid (found in his daughter's home in the compound).

Despite the public's anger, Qaddafi's family continued to issue statements of loyalty to him. A few weeks earlier, son Saif had condemned the NATO strikes with some of his father's bluster: "[Libya] is a piece of cake: rich, full of gas, oil.... Listen, NATO and rebels both are in a hurry, they want to finish as soon as possible because they are hungry, they are tired, they want to share the cake.... For them, Libya is like fast food, like McDonald's."[58] On October 10, daughter Aisha Qaddafi offered more staunch support: "The man is the man. He never changes his principles. He believes in causes, defending the poor and the underdog."[59]

Death of a Dictator

Qaddafi's end was sudden and brutal. On October 20, NATO planes attacked a convoy of SUVs on the desert road heading out of Sirte, apparently unaware that Muammar Qaddafi was inside. Rebel troops moved in to capture the occupants of the damaged vehicles, who were fleeing on foot. They found the dictator, dirty, disheveled, and disoriented but alive, hiding in a drainage pipe.

The next chaotic minutes were captured in clips of cell phone video. Shouting, disorganized fighters dragged Qaddafi from his hiding place. More fighters rushed to the scene and beat the now-bloodied Qaddafi, with rifles and sticks. Stumbling, reportedly begging his captors for his life, his last words were, ironically, "Do you know right from wrong?"[60] Qaddafi was killed shortly after by gunshot wounds to the head and chest. His body was draped on the hood of a car. Jubilant rebels fired automatic weapons into the air. Later that day it was revealed that Qaddafi's son Mutassim had been captured and killed in Sirte that same morning.

Qaddafi's body was accorded no dignities. So that Libyans could see for themselves the hated dictator was really dead, the NTC lay his stripped corpse on the floor of an industrial freezer in Misrata and opened the site for four days of public viewing. On October 25, Qaddafi was buried in an undisclosed, apparently unmarked desert location.

Qaddafi's death makes front-page news in the International Herald Tribune. Qaddafi was killed on October 20, 2011 by rebel forces.

Qaddafi's Last Will and Testament

In the days immediately following the death of Qaddafi, the Arabic-language daily newspaper *Asharq Alawsat* released a transcript of what it claimed was the Libyan dictator's last will and testament. The document was reportedly written in Sirte on October 17, 2011, and handed to relatives, who first published the will on a pro-Qaddafi website.

In the document, Qaddafi asks to be buried in the Qaddafi family plot in Sirte. He asks that his family be treated well, and then he calls on loyalists to continue the fight against NATO and the NTC:

> I call on my supporters to continue the resistance, and fight any foreign aggressor against Libya, today, tomorrow and always.
>
> Let the free people of the world know that I could have sold out our cause in return for a secure and stable personal life. I received many offers to this effect but chose to be at the vanguard of confrontation as a badge of duty and honour. Even if we do not win immediately, we will provide a lesson to future generations that choosing to protect the nation is an honour and selling it out is the greatest betrayal that history will forever remember, however they try to portray this.

Quoted in Sawsan Abu-Husain and Khaled Mahmoud. "Gaddafi: The Last Will and Testament." *Asharq Alawsat*, October 23, 2011. www.asharq-e.com/news. asp?section=3&id=27056.

Qaddafi's Legacy

Qaddafi left behind no lasting institutions that could keep Libya running in his absence. He was so effective in eliminating opposition that there is no ideology or party or clear successor to replace him. The rebel alliance that brought him down is united by little except their hatred of their former leader. It is likely, therefore that a range of rivals will try to fill the power vacuum: Islamists, monarchists, democrats, tribal leaders all have their own ideas about the kind of state Libya should become.

Libyan political writer Hisham Matar spoke for many who hope that whatever form of government comes next, it is not established through violence: "We have defeated Gaddafi on the battlefield, now we must defeat him in our imagination. We must not allow his legacy to corrupt our dream. Let's keep focused on the true prize: unity, democracy and the rule of law. Let's not seek revenge; that would diminish our future.

… We have got rid of Muammar Gaddafi. Now the building starts."[61]

Introduction: Who Was the Real Qaddafi?

1. Daniel Kawczynski. *Seeking Gaddafi: Libya, the West, and the Arab Spring.* London: Biteback, 2011. Kindle ed., loc. 1666.
2. Kawczynski. *Seeking Gaddafi,* loc. 1676.

Chapter 1: A Child of Poverty in a Family of Wanderers

3. Mirella Bianco. *Gadafi: Voice from the Desert.* London: Longman, 1975, p. 4.
4. Quoted in Revolutionary Committee Movement. "Muammar al Qadhafi: The Consummate Revolutionary Leader of the World Revolution." Mathaba.net, n.d. www.mathaba.net/info/mqadhafi.htm.
5. Geoff Simons. *Libya: The Struggle for Survival.* 2nd ed. New York: St. Martin's, 1996, p. 170.
6. Simons. *Libya,* p. 170.
7. Quoted in Revolutionary Committee Movement. "Muammar al Qadhafi."
8. Quoted in David Blundy and Andrew Lycett. *Qaddafi and the Libyan Revolution.* London: Weidenfeld and Nicolson, 1987, p. 40.
9. Quoted in Blundy and Lycett. *Qaddafi and the Libyan Revolution,* p. 42.
10. Quoted in Blundy and Lycett. *Qaddafi and the Libyan Revolution,* p. 43.
11. Quoted in Blundy and Lycett. *Qaddafi and the Libyan Revolution,* p. 40.
12. Quoted in Blundy and Lycett. *Qaddafi and the Libyan Revolution,* pp. 40-41.

Chapter 2: The Making of a Revolutionary

13. Quoted in Blundy and Lycett. *Qaddafi and the Libyan Revolution,* p. 45.
14. Quoted in Blundy and Lycett. *Qaddafi and the Libyan Revolution,* p. 46.

15. Lillian Craig Harris. *Libya: Qadhafi's Revolution and the Modern State*. Boulder, CO: Westview, 1986, pp. 51–52.
16. Quoted in Blundy and Lycett. *Qaddafi and the Libyan Revolution*, p. 49.

Chapter 3: Building a Dictatorship

17. Quoted in Geoff Simons. *Libya: The Struggle for Survival*. New York: Palgrave Macmillan, 1993, p. 179.
18. Quoted in Simons. *Libya*, p. 179.
19. Quoted in Simons, *Libya*, p. 179.
20. Ron McWhorter, e-mail interview with Sheila Wyborny, July 12, 2011.
21. Dirk Vandewalle. "Dirk Vandewalle Peers Inside Gadhafi's World: Interview with Dirk Vandewalle." By Terry Gross. *Fresh Air*, National Public Radio, February 28, 2011. www.npr.org/2011/02/28/134132726/dirk-vandewalle-peers-inside-qaddafis-world.
22. Quoted in John L. Wright. *Libya: A Modern History*. Baltimore: Johns Hopkins University Press, 1982, p. 179.
23. Quoted in Kawczynski. *Seeking Gaddafi*, loc. 4017.
24. Michael Cullen, e-mail interview with Sheila Wyborny, July 17, 2011.
25. Quoted in Mohamed Eljahmi, "Libya and the U.S.: Qadhafi Unrepentant." *Middle East Quarterly*, Winter 2006. www.meforum.org/878/libya-and-the-us-qadhafi-unrepentant.

Chapter 4: Rogue Leader of a Rogue Nation

26. Quoted in Eljahmi, "Libya and the U.S."
27. Amnesty International. "Libya: Serious Human Rights Violations amid Secrecy and Isolation," June 25, 1997. www.amnesty.org/en/library/asset/MDE19/011/1997/en/5bd275f4-ea52-11dd-965c-b55c1122d73f/mde190111997en.html.
28. Quoted in Kawczynski. *Seeking Gaddafi*, loc. 4197.
29. Eljahmi, "Libya and the U.S."
30. Quoted in Kawczynski. *Seeking Gaddafi*, loc. 2166.
31. *Newsweek*. "Kaddafi: The Most Dangerous Man in the World?" Cover story. July 20, 1981.
32. Ronald Reagan, White House press conference, April 9, 1986. www.presidency.ucsb.edu/ws/index.php?pid=37105#axzz1gyirqHZ6.

33. Quoted in Kawczynski. *Seeking Gaddafi,* loc. 2379.
34. Ronald Reagan, nationally televised press conference, April 15, 1986. Quoted at www.upi.com/Audio/Year_in_ Review/Events-of-1986/Strike-on-Qaddafi-and-Soviet- Espionage/12297050136623-4/.
35. Quoted in Kawczynski. *Seeking Gaddafi,* loc. 2357.
36. Quoted in Kawczynski. *Seeking Gaddafi,* loc. 4207.

Chapter 5: Qaddafi Comes In from the Cold

37. Quoted in Kawczynski. *Seeking Gaddafi,* loc. 3311.
38. Quoted in Kawczynski. *Seeking Gaddafi,* loc. 162.
39. Krista Bremer. "Leaving Libya: How I Learned to Appreciate Everything I'd Taken for Granted." *O: The Oprah Magazine,* July 2011. www.oprah.com/spirit/Women-in-Libya-Hoping- for-Freedom-in-Libya.
40. Quoted in Kawczynski. *Seeking Gaddafi,* loc. 3094.
41. Muammar Qaddafi. "The One-State Solution." *New York Times,* January 21, 2009. www.nytimes.com/2009/01/22/ opinion/22qaddafi.html.
42. Helena Bachman. "Gaddafi's Oddest Idea: Abolish Switzerland." *Time,* September 25, 2009. www.time.com/ time/world/article/0,8599,1926053,00.html.
43. Ed Pilkington. "UN General Assembly: 100 minutes in the Life of Muammar Gaddafi." *Guardian,* September 23, 2009. www .guardian.co.uk/world/2009/sep/23/gaddafi-un-speech.
44. Quoted in Chuck Bennett and Jeremy Olshan. "Translator Collapsed During Kadhafi's Rambling Diatribe." *New York Post,* September 24, 2009. www.nypost.com/p/news/international/translator_ collapsed_during_khadafy_EAHR9j2jHOt8Y6TFRhrcQM.
45. Quoted in Kawczynski. *Seeking Gaddafi,* loc. 105.
46. Vandewalle. "Vandewall Peers Inside Gadhafi's World."

Chapter 6: The Bloody End of a Tyrant

47. Jon Lee Anderson. "King of Kings." *New Yorker,* November 7, 2011, p. 44.
48. Quoted in Christiane Amanpour. "'My People Love Me.'" ABC News, February 28, 2011. http://abcnews.go.com/ International/christiane-amanpour-interviews-libyas-moammar -gadhafi/story?id=13019942.

49. Quoted in BBC News: Africa. "Libya: Gaddafi Offers Talks with NATO." April 30, 2011. www.bbc.co.uk/news/world-africa-13247399.
50. Quoted in Al-Arabiya News. "Everything Will Be Over in 48 Hours: Gaddafi's Son." March 16, 2011. www.alarabiya .net/articles/2011/03/16/141846.html.
51. The Libyan Interim National Council. www.ntclibya.org/english/.
52. Quoted in Dan Murphy. "Qaddafi Counteroffensive Is Closing World's Window to Aid Libya Rebels." *Christian Science Monitor*, March 10, 2011. www.csmonitor.com/World/Middle-East/2011/0310/Qaddafi-counteroffensive-is-closing-world-s-window-to-aid-Libya-rebels.
53. The Libyan Interim National Council.
54. Robert Dreyfus. "The Fall of Qaddafi." *Nation,* August 22, 2011. www.thenation.com/blog/162891/fall-qaddafi.
55. Quoted in MSNBC.com: Mideast and North Africa. "US, Other Western Nations Declare Gadhafi Regime No Longer Legitimate," July 15, 2011. www.msnbc.com/id/43765510/ns/world_news-mideast_n_africa/.
56. Quoted in Kareem Fahim. "Libyan Rebels in Zawiyah Threaten Supply Line to Tripoli." *New York Times,* August 14, 2011. www.nytimes.com/2011/08/15/world/africa/15libya.html.
57. Quoted in Martin Evans. "Libya: The Hunt Is On for Col. Gaddafi," *Daily Telegraph* (London), August 22, 2011. www.telegraph.co.uk/news/worldnews/africaand-indianocean/libya/8716572/Libya-the-hunt-is-on-for-Col-Gaddafi.html.
58. Quoted in Dan Amira. "How the War in Libya Is Like Fast Food," *New York,* July 1, 2011. http://nymag.com/daily/intel/2011/07/qaddafi_warns_nato_we_can_deci.html.
59. Quoted in Colin Freeman. "Gaddafi's Girl a Chip Off the Old Block." *Sunday Telegraph* (London), October 10, 2010. http://www.telegraph.co.uk/news/worldnews/africaandindianocean/libya/8053181/Meet-Gaddafis-girl-a-chip-off-the-old-block.html.
60. Quoted in David Williams. "Who Shot Gaddafi?" *Daily Mail* (London), October 21, 2011. www.dailymail.co.uk/news/

article-2051361/GADDAFI-DEAD-VIDEO-Dictator-begs-life-summary-execution.html.

62. Hisham Matar. "Gaddafi Is Gone: Long Live Unity, Democracy, and the Rule of Law." *Guardian* (Manchester, UK), August 22, 2011. www.guardian.co.uk/commentisfree/2011/aug/22/libya-gaddafi-tripoli-hisham-matar.

1942(?)

Muammar Qaddafi is born on June 7 south of Sirte, Libya.

1959

Oil is discovered in the Libyan desert, marking the beginning of Libya's oil industry and investment in exploration and production facilities by foreign oil companies.

1963

Graduates from secondary school in Misrata after being expelled from other schools for inciting political protests.

1965

Graduates from Benghazi Military Academy as a lieutenant in the Libyan Army; attends six-month Signal Corps training program in England.

1969

September 1, heads military coup that topples the monarchy, to be replaced by Revolutionary Command Council (RCC); October 29, demands withdrawal of all British troops and bases.

1970

Orders American military troops and bases to leave Libya; nationalizes oil works of foreign oil companies, all banks; reorganizes Libya into small districts to break down traditional tribal boundaries. September 28, Qaddafi's hero Nasser dies, marking the end of good relations between Libya and Egypt.

1971

Creates General People's Congress (GPC); creates Federation of Arab Republics (FAR), a limited, partial Arab union among Libya, Egypt, and Sudan; nationalizes all insurance companies and abolishes the right to strike.

1973

April 15, delivers so-called five-point address in Zuwarah, assumes absolute power; December 17, Rome airport massacre carried out by Palestinian terrorists who claim to be acting on direct orders of Qaddafi.

1976–1979

The Green Book is published in three volumes.

1977

Renames Libya the Great Socialist People's Libyan Arab Jamahiriyya; resigns as secretary-general of the GPC (from this point on, calls himself merely a guide to the nation, a figurehead with no formal power); U.S. Defense Department adds Libya to list of potential enemies of the United States; Libya-Egypt border clashes lead to dissolving of FAR.

1978–1987

Goes to war with Chad over disputed Aouzou Strip.

1978

Sets out to abolish all private property, all privately owned retail and private business/trading, all savings accounts.

1979

Dissolves RCC; converts Libyan embassies abroad into People's Bureaus; December 2, attack on U.S. embassy in Tripoli; December 29, U.S. State Department lists Libya as sponsor of state terrorism.

1980–1981

United States and Libya end diplomatic relations. Qaddafi calls for assassination of expatriate opponents ("stray dogs"), creates Arab passports and opens borders to all Arabs.

1982

United States bans all exports to Libya, except medicines and food, and all imports of Libyan oil; orders Americans working in Libya to return home.

1984

Britain breaks off relations with Libya after Qaddafi orders Libyan embassy personnel in London to fire on peaceful demonstrators, killing a British policewoman.

1985

December 27, coordinated terrorist attacks at Rome and Vienna airports, publicly praised by Qaddafi as justified retaliation to Israeli attacks on PLO headquarters. President Reagan strengthens embargo on goods to and from Libya, freezes Libyan assets in U.S. banks.

1986

Bombing of West Berlin nightclub on April 5, allegedly ordered by Qaddafi, kills two U.S. soldiers; Reagan calls Qaddafi the "mad dog of the Middle East" at April 9 news conference; U.S. air attack on Tripoli and Benghazi on April 15.

1987

Economic hardship and reduced oil profits force Qaddafi to allow reintroduction of private business, announce agricultural and judicial reforms, end hostilities with Chad while claiming Aouzou Strip as Libyan territory.

1988

December 21, Pan Am Flight 103 explodes over Lockerbie, Scotland.

1989

January 4, U.S. Air Force downs two Libyan fighters over the Gulf of Sidra; September 19, French airline UTA Flight 772 explodes over Niger.

1991

Libya is indicted in connection with Lockerbie bombing; two Libyans charged with bombing on Qaddafi's orders.

1992–1993

United Nations Resolution 748 orders Qaddafi to turn over Lockerbie bombing suspects; UN Resolution 883 imposes harsh sanctions, freezes Libyan assets overseas, bans export of spare parts for oil industry into Libya.

1994

International Court of Justice awards disputed Aouzou strip to Chad; Qaddafi loyalists put down military rebellion in Misrata.

2003

Qaddafi renounces Libyan weapons of mass destruction programs.

2004

Agrees to pay compensation to victims of the 1986 West Berlin nightclub bombing and families of Lockerbie bombing victims; majority of U.S. sanctions against Libya lifted.

2008

U.S.-Libya diplomatic relations restored, leading to reopening of U.S. embassy in Tripoli.

2009

Qaddafi addresses United Nations.

2011

Arab Spring: Democracy movements topple Mubarak of Egypt and Ben Ali of Tunisia, threaten authoritarian regimes in Syria and Yemen. Uprising begins in Libya in February, centered in Benghazi and organized as the National Transitional Council (NTC). NATO military intervention begins March 19; Tripoli falls to rebel forces August 22; Qaddafi is captured and killed outside Sirte by NTC forces on October 20.

For More Information

Books

David Blundy and Andrew Lycett. *Qaddafi and the Libyan Revolution*. Boston: Little, Brown, 1987. For a more mature reader, this volume profiles Muammar Qaddafi's rise from poverty to rock star status and features his ties to terrorism.

Henry M. Christmas, ed. *Qaddafi's Green Book: An Unauthorized Edition*. Buffalo, NY: Prometheus Books, 1988. With a lengthy introduction to the man and his country, this book contains all three parts of Qaddafi's Green Book, his model for government and society. Suitable for students at higher reading levels.

Daniel Kawczynski. *Seeking Gaddafi: Libya, the West, and the Arab Spring*. London: Biteback, 2011. A straightforward, insightful discussion of Qaddafi and his entire regime, by a member of Parliament and the adviser on Libyan affairs to the British Foreign Office.

Brenda Lange. *Muammar Qaddafi*. Philadelphia: Chelsea House, 2005. A concise but comprehensive biography about Qaddafi, his background, and his regime.

Periodicals

Jon Lee Anderson. "King of Kings." *New Yorker,* November 7, 2011, pp. 44–57.

Mohamed Eljahmi. "Libya and the U.S.: Qadhafi Unrepentant." *Middle East Quarterly,* Winter 2006, pp. 11–20.

Paul Richter. "As Libya Takes Stock, Moammar Kadafi's Hidden Riches Astound." *Los Angeles Times,* October 21, 2011.

Internet Sources

Christiane Amanpour, "'My People Love Me,'" ABC News, February 28, 2011. http://abcnews.go.com/International/christiane-amanpour-interviews-libyas-moammar-gadhafi/story?id=13019942.

Sadie Bass. "How Many Different Ways Can You Spell 'Gaddafi'?" ABC News, September 22, 2009. http://abcnews.go.com/blogs/headlines/2009/09/how-many-different-ways-can-you-spell-gaddafi/.

Daniel Byman and Matthew Waxman, "Libyan Limbo: Six Reasons Why It's Been So Tough to Get Qaddafi to Quit." *Foreign Policy*, June 2, 2011. www.foreignpolicy.com/articles/2011/06/02/libyan_limbo.

Howard French. "How Qaddafi Reshaped Africa." *Atlantic,* March 1, 2011. www.theatlantic.com/international/archive/2011/03/how-qaddafi-reshaped-africa/71861/.

Tim Gaynor and Taha Zargoun. "Gaddafi's Death: Who Pulled the Trigger?" Reuters, October 20, 2011. www.reuters.com/article/2011/10/20/us-libya-gaddafi-finalhours-idUSTRE79J5Q720111020.

Guardian (Manchester, UK). "Libyan Rebels Raid Gaddafi Family Mansions—in Pictures." August 25, 2011. www.guardian.co.uk/world/gallery/2011/aug/25/libyan-gaddafi-mansions-in-pictures.

Hisham Matar. "Gaddafi Is Gone. Long Live Unity, Democracy and the Rule of Law." *Guardian* (Manchester, UK), August 22, 2011. www.guardian.co.uk/commentisfree/2011/aug/22/libya-gaddafi-tripoli-hisham-matar.

Nicholas Hegel McClelland. "Gaddafi Fashion: The Emperor Had Some Crazy Clothes." *Time*, October 22, 2011. www.time.com/time/photogallery/0,29307,2055860,00.html.

Jason Pack. "Qaddafi's Legacy." *Foreign Policy,* October 20, 2011. www.foreignpolicy.com/articles/2011/10/20/qaddafi_s_legacy.

David Poort. "Libyans Turn Page on Gaddafi's 'Green Book.'" Al Jazeera, September 14, 2011. http://english.aljazeera.net/news/africa/2011/09/20119141151017195.html.

Nissa Rhee. "Libya Corruption, Cult of Personality Drive Qaddafi's Grip on Power." *Christian Science Monitor,* February 23, 2011. www.csmonitor.com/World/terrorism-security/2011/0223/Libya-corruption-cult-of-personality-drive-Qaddafi-s-grip-on-power-WikiLeaks-cable.

Dirk Vandewalle. "Dirk Vandewalle Peers Inside Gadhafi's World: Interview with Dirk Vandewalle." By Terry Gross. *Fresh Air,* National Public Radio, February 28, 2011. www.npr

.org/2011/02/28/134132726/dirk-vandewalle-peers-inside-qaddafis-world.

Dirk Vandewalle. "Libya Since 1969." Command Posts, Focus On: Intel, March 25, 2011. www.commandposts.com/2011/03/libya-since-1969/.

Websites

The Great Socialist People's Libyan Arab Jamahiriya (www .mathaba.net/info/). The official website of Qaddafi's loyalist government.

The Libyan Republic, National Transitional Council (www .ntclibya.org/english/). This is the website of the opposition forces, recognized by most countries as Libya's legitimate government.

Sheila Wyborny has authored several titles in Lucent's *People in the News* series, including *Kim Jong Il* and *Dwayne Johnson*. Viqi Wagner is a legislative editor and writer with a special interest in international politics. She lives and works in Richmond, Virginia.